# Bahá'í Marriage
and Family Life

# Bahá'í Marriage and Family Life

## Selections from the Writings of the Bahá'í Faith

Bahá'í Publishing Trust
Wilmette, Illinois 60091

Originally published by the National Spiritual Assembly
of the Bahá'ís of Canada, 1983

Reprinted by permission in 1997 by the
U.S. Bahá'í Publishing Trust,
Wilmette, IL 60091-2844

Printed in the United States of America

00  99  98  97      4  3  2  1

### Library of Congress Cataloging-in-Publication Data

Bahá'í marriage and family life : selections from the writings of the
   Bahá'í Faith.
        p.   cm.
       Originally published: Thornhill, Ont., Canada : National Spiritual
Assembly of the Bahá'ís of Canada, 1983.
       Includes bibliographical references.
       ISBN 0-87743-258-9
       1. Marriage—Religious aspects—Bahai Faith. 2. Bahai Faith—
Doctrines. 3. Family—Religious aspects—Bahai faith.
BP388.M37B34    1997
297.9'3441—dc21

                                  97–60
                                 CIP

# Table of Contents

# Introduction

All of the institutions of the Bahá'í Faith were established so that love and unity would have means of expression in the life of human society. This is especially true of the institution of marriage, which Bahá'u'lláh called a "fortress for well-being," and which is the foundation of family life.

Nothing is more delightful than to visualize ourselves as entering into a relationship which 'Abdu'l-Bahá describes as "mutual attraction of mind and heart," "a tie that will endure forever," enabling us to become "loving companions and comrades," and "at one with each other for time and eternity." The question is not: "Is this what I want?" The question is: "Have we developed the qualities of character which will make it possible to build such a relationship?"

This compilation is designed to help us prepare for marriage, to assist those of us already married, and to improve our family life. It is also intended to assist Bahá'í Spiritual Assemblies in their educational and counseling responsibilities.

Two compilations from the Bahá'í teachings on "Discouraging Divorce" and "Family Life," sent to National Spiritual Assemblies by the Universal House of Justice, have been incorporated into this collection. Additional passages have been selected for their capacity to shed further light on the terms and concepts referred to in the guidance specifically related to Bahá'í marriage and family life.

What greater joy is there than to love and to be loved, and to raise a family distinguished for its unity and harmony? What effort is too great, what discipline too strenuous for the reward of such a joy?

Warmest Bahá'í love,

NATIONAL SPIRITUAL ASSEMBLY
OF THE BAHÁ'ÍS OF CANADA

# Bahá'í Marriage
# and Family Life

# I. THE INSTITUTION OF MARRIAGE

## A. Law of Marriage

**1.** "And when He desired to manifest grace and beneficence to men, and to set the world in order, He revealed observances and created laws; among them He established the law of marriage, made it as a fortress for well-being and salvation, and enjoined it upon us in that which was sent down out of the heaven of sanctity in His Most Holy Book. He saith, great is His glory: 'Enter into wedlock, O people, that ye may bring forth one who will make mention of Me and My servants. This is My bidding unto you; hold fast to it as an assistance to yourselves.'"

(Bahá'u'lláh, *Bahá'í Prayers*, U.S. 1982, p. 187)

**2.** "The pious deeds of the monks and priests among the followers of the Spirit—upon Him be the peace of God—are remembered in His presence. In this Day, however, let them give up the life of seclusion and direct their steps towards the open world and busy themselves with that

3

which will profit themselves and others. We have granted them leave to enter into wedlock that they may bring forth one who will make mention of God, the Lord of the seen and the unseen, the Lord of the Exalted Throne."

(Bahá'u'lláh, *Tablets of Bahá'u'lláh*, p. 24)

**3.** "Regarding the question of matrimony: Know thou that the command of marriage is eternal. It will never be changed nor altered. This is divine creation and there is not the slightest possibility that change or alteration affect this divine creation (marriage)."

('Abdu'l-Bahá, *Tablets of Abdul-Baha Abbas*, Vol. II, p. 474)

**4.** "Of course, under normal circumstances, every person should consider it his moral duty to marry. And this is what Bahá'u'lláh has encouraged the believers to do. But marriage is by no means an obligation. In the last resort it is for the individual to decide whether he wishes to lead a family life or live in a state of celibacy."

(Shoghi Effendi, from a letter dated May 3, 1936, to an individual believer)

**5.** "It should, moreover, be borne in mind that although to be married is highly desirable, and Bahá'u'lláh has strongly recommended it, it is not the central purpose of life. If a person has to wait a considerable period before finding a spouse, or if ultimately, he or she must remain single, it does not mean that he or she is thereby unable to fulfill his or her life's purpose."

(Universal House of Justice, *Messages from the Universal House of Justice, 1963–1986*, 126.9)

## B. Commitments and Responsibilities

**6.** "Bahá'í marriage is the commitment of the two parties one to the other, and their mutual attachment of mind and heart. Each must, however, exercise the utmost care to become thoroughly acquainted with the character of the other, that the binding covenant between them may be a tie that will endure forever. Their purpose must be this: to become loving companions and comrades and at one with each other for time and eternity. . .

"The true marriage of Bahá'ís is this, that husband and wife should be united both physically and spiritually, that they may ever improve the spiritual life of each other, and may enjoy everlasting unity throughout all the worlds of God. This is Bahá'í marriage."

('Abdu'l-Bahá, *Selections from the Writings of 'Abdu'l-Bahá*, 86.1–2)

**7.** "O ye two believers in God! The Lord, peerless is He, hath made woman and man to abide with each other in the closest companionship, and to be even as a single soul. They are two helpmates, two intimate friends, who should be concerned about the welfare of each other.

"If they live thus, they will pass through this world with perfect contentment, bliss, and peace of heart, and become the object of divine grace and favor in the Kingdom of heaven. But if they do other than this they will live out their lives in great bitterness, longing at every moment for death, and will be shamefaced in the heavenly realm.

"Strive, then, to abide, heart and soul with each other as two doves in the nest, for this is to be blessed in both worlds."

('Abdu'l-Bahá, *Selections from the Writings of 'Abdu'l-Bahá*, 92.1–3)

**8.** "O ye my two beloved children! The news of your union, as soon as it reached me, imparted infinite joy and gratitude. Praise be to God, those two faithful birds have sought shelter in one nest. I beseech God that He may enable them to raise an honored family, for the importance of marriage lieth in the bringing up of a richly blessed family, so that with entire gladness they may, even as candles, illuminate the world. For the enlightenment of the world dependeth upon the existence of man. If man did not exist in this world, it would have been like a tree without fruit. My hope is that you both may become even as one tree, and may, through the outpourings of the cloud of loving-kindness, acquire freshness and charm, and may blossom and yield fruit, so that your line may eternally endure.

"Upon ye be the Glory of the Most Glorious."

('Abdu'l-Bahá, *Selections from the Writings of 'Abdu'l-Bahá*, 88.1–2)

9. ". . . it is enjoined upon the father and mother, as a duty, to strive with all effort to train the daughter and the son, to nurse them from the breast of knowledge and to rear them in the bosom of sciences and arts. Should they neglect this matter, they shall be held responsible and worthy of reproach in the presence of the stern Lord."

('Abdu'l-Bahá, *Selections from the Writings of 'Abdu'l-Bahá,* 98.2)

10. "There is nothing in the Sacred Writings specifically on the subjects of birth control, abortion or sterilization, but Bahá'u'lláh did state that the primary purpose of marriage was the procreation of children, and it is to this primary purpose that the beloved Guardian alludes in many of the letters which are quoted in the compilation. This does not imply that a couple are obliged to have as many children as they can; the Guardian's secretary clearly stated on his behalf, in answer to an enquiry, that it was for the husband and wife to decide how many children they would have. A decision to have no children at all would vitiate the primary purpose of marriage unless, of course, there were some medical reason why such a decision would be required."

(Universal House of Justice, from a letter dated January 28, 1977,
to an individual believer)

## C. The Marriage Ceremony

11. "It is incumbent upon both parties to recite a specifically revealed verse indicating their being content with the will of God."
(*Synopsis and Codification of the Laws and Ordinances of the Kitáb-i-Aqdas,* p. 40)

12. "The specifically revealed verse is, 'We will all, verily, abide by the Will of God.'"
(*Synopsis and Codification of the Laws and Ordinances of the Kitáb-i-Aqdas,* p. 59)

13. ". . . Bahá'í marriages should be referred to Assemblies to officiate."
(Shoghi Effendi, from a letter dated June 23, 1950,
written on his behalf to the National Spiritual Assembly of Canada)

**14.** "The ceremony itself must be very simple."
(Shoghi Effendi, quoted in *Principles of Bahá'í Administration*, p. 13)

**15.** "Bahá'í marriage should at present not be pressed into any kind of a uniform mold. What is absolutely essential is what Bahá'u'lláh stipulated in the Aqdas: the friends can add to these selected writings if they please—but the so-called 'Marriage Tablet' (revealed by 'Abdu'l-Bahá) is not a necessary part of every Bahá'í marriage."
(Shoghi Effendi, quoted in *Principles of Bahá'í Administration*, p. 14)

**16.** "In cases where there is more than one ceremony, the Bahá'í service and the other civil or religious ceremony must be performed on the same day."
(Shoghi Effendi, from a letter dated June 20, 1940, to the National Spiritual Assembly of Australia and New Zealand)

**17.** "As to the holding of the Bahá'í and civil ceremonies on the same day, as consummation of the marriage should not take place until both ceremonies have been held, a night should not intervene between the two ceremonies."
(Universal House of Justice, from a letter dated April 23, 1971, to the National Spiritual Assembly of the United States)

**18.** ". . . The bride and groom, before two witnesses, must state: 'We will all, verily, abide by the Will of God.' These two witnesses may be chosen by the couple or by the Spiritual Assembly, but must in any case be acceptable to the Assembly."
(Universal House of Justice, from a letter dated August 8, 1969, to the National Spiritual Assembly of the United States)

**19.** "The consummation of marriage by a couple is, as you aptly state, an intimate and private matter outside the scrutiny of others. While consummation normally implies a sexual relationship, the Bahá'í law requiring consummation to take place within twenty-four hours of the

ceremony can be considered as fulfilled if the couple has commenced cohabitation with the intention of setting up the family relationship."
(Universal House of Justice, from a letter dated July 28, 1978,
to an individual believer)

20. ". . . persons wishing to marry after they become Bahá'ís must have a Bahá'í ceremony and are indeed not regarded as married unless they have met the requirements of Bahá'í law."
(Universal House of Justice, from a letter dated May 22, 1967,
to the National Spiritual Assembly of the United States)

21. ". . . as the Guardian says, 'Bahá'í marriage is something you perform when you are going to be united for the first time, not long after the union takes place.' If, however, such a couple would like to have a meeting of their friends at which Bahá'í prayers and readings are said on behalf of their marriage now that they are Bahá'ís, there is no objection to their doing so, although it must be understood that this does not constitute a Bahá'í marriage ceremony."
(Universal House of Justice, from a letter dated June 23, 1969,
to the National Spiritual Assembly of Peru)

## D. Marriage as the Basis of Unity

22. "The Great Being saith: O ye children of men! The fundamental purpose animating the Faith of God and His Religion is to safeguard the interests and promote the unity of the human race, and to foster the spirit of love and fellowship amongst men."
(Bahá'u'lláh, *Gleanings from the Writings of Bahá'u'lláh*, p. 215)

23. ". . . Verily they are married in obedience to Thy command. Cause them to become the signs of harmony and unity until the end of time. Verily Thou art the Omnipotent, the Omnipresent and the Almighty!"
('Abdu'l-Bahá, *Bahá'í Prayers*, U.S. 1982, p. 107)

**24.** "From separation doth every kind of hurt and harm proceed, but the union of created things doth ever yield most laudable results. From the pairing of even the smallest particles in the world of being are the grace and bounty of God made manifest; and the higher the degree, the more momentous is the union. 'Glory be to Him Who hath created all the pairs, of such things as earth produceth, and out of men themselves, and of things beyond their ken.' And above all other unions is that between human beings, especially when it cometh to pass in the love of God. Thus is the primal oneness made to appear; thus is laid the foundation of love in the spirit."

('Abdu'l-Bahá, *Selections from the Writings of 'Abdu'l-Bahá*, 87.2)

**25.** "Marriage, among the mass of the people, is a physical bond, and this union can only be temporary, since it is foredoomed to a physical separation at the close.

"Among the people of Bahá, however, marriage must be a union of the body and of the spirit as well, for here both husband and wife are aglow with the same wine, both are enamored of the same matchless Face, both live and move through the same spirit, both are illumined by the same glory. This connection between them is a spiritual one, hence it is a bond that will abide forever. Likewise do they enjoy strong and lasting ties in the physical world as well, for if the marriage is based both on the spirit and the body, that union is a true one, hence it will endure. If, however, the bond is physical and nothing more, it is sure to be only temporary, and must inexorably end in separation.

"When, therefore, the people of Bahá undertake to marry, the union must be a true relationship, a spiritual coming together as well as a physical one, so that throughout every phase of life, and in all the worlds of God, their union will endure; for this real oneness is a gleaming out of the love of God.

"In the same way, when any souls grow to be true believers, they will attain a spiritual relationship with one another, and show forth a tenderness which is not of this world. They will, all of them, become elated from a draught of divine love, and that union of theirs, that connection, will also abide forever. Souls, that is, who will consign their own selves to oblivion, strip from themselves the defects of humankind, and unchain themselves from human bondage, will beyond any doubt be illumined with the heavenly splendors of oneness, and will all attain unto real union in the world that dieth not."

(‘Abdu’l-Bahá, *Selections from the Writings of ‘Abdu’l-Bahá*, 84.2–5)


26.  "As to thy question concerning the husband and wife, the tie between them and the children given to them by God: Know thou, verily, the husband is one who hath sincerely turned unto God, is awakened by the call of the Beauty of the All-Glorious and chanteth the verses of Oneness in the great assemblies; the wife is a being who wisheth to be overflowing with and seeketh after the attributes of God and His names; and the tie between them is none other than the Word of God. Verily, it causeth the multitudes to assemble together and the remote ones to be united. Thus the husband and wife are brought into affinity, are united and harmonized, even as though they were one person. Through their mutual union, companionship and love great results are produced in the world, both material and spiritual. The spiritual result is the appearance of divine bounties. The material result is the children who are born in the cradle of the love of God, who are nurtured by the breast of the knowledge of God, who are brought up in the bosom of the gift of God, and who are fostered in the lap of the training of God. Such children are those of whom it was said by Christ, 'Verily, they are the children of the Kingdom!'"

(‘Abdu’l-Bahá, *Tablets of Abdul-Baha Abbas*, Vol. III, pp. 605–606)


## E. Attitude Towards Divorce

27.  "God doth verily love union and concord, and abhorreth separation and divorce."

(Bahá'u'lláh, quoted in a compilation dated January 18, 1980,
sent by the Universal House of Justice to National Spiritual Assemblies)


28.  "Now the friends in America must live and conduct themselves in this way. They must strictly refrain from divorce unless something ariseth which compelleth them to separate because of their aver-

sion for each other, in that case with the knowledge of the Spiritual Assembly they may decide to separate. They must then be patient and wait one complete year. If during this year harmony is not re-established between them, then divorce may be realized. It should not happen that upon the occurrence of a slight friction or displeasure between husband and wife, the husband would think of union with some other woman, or God forbid, the wife also think of another husband. This is contrary to the standard of heavenly value and true chastity. The friends of God must so live and conduct themselves, and evince such excellence of character and conduct, as to make others astonished. The love between husband and wife should not be purely physical, nay rather it must be spiritual and heavenly. These two souls should be considered as one soul. How difficult it would be to divide a single soul! Nay, greater would be the difficulty.

"In short, the foundation of the Kingdom of God is based upon harmony and love, oneness, relationship and union, not upon differences, especially between husband and wife. If one of these two become the cause of divorce, that one will unquestionably fall into great difficulties, will become the victim of formidable calamities and experience deep remorse."

('Abdu'l-Bahá, quoted in a compilation dated January 18, 1980,<br>sent by the Universal House of Justice to National Spiritual Assemblies)

**29.** "The situation facing you is admittedly difficult and delicate, but no less grave and indeed vital are the responsibilities which it entails and which, as a faithful and loyal believer, you should conscientiously and thoroughly assume. The Guardian, therefore, while fully alive to the special circumstances of your case, and however profound his sympathy may be for you in this challenging issue with which you are so sadly faced, cannot, in view of the emphatic injunctions contained in the Teachings, either sanction your demand to contract a second marriage while your first wife is still alive and is united with you in the sacred bonds of matrimony, or even suggest or approve that you divorce her just in order to be permitted to marry a new one.

"For the Bahá'í Teachings do not only preclude the possibility of bigamy, but also, while permitting divorce, consider it a reprehensible act, which should be resorted to only in exceptional circumstances, and when grave issues are involved, transcending such . . . considerations as physical attraction or sexual compatibility and harmony. The institution of marriage, as established by Bahá'u'lláh, while giving due importance to the physical aspect of marital union considers it as subordinate to the moral and spiritual purposes and functions with which it has been invested by an all-wise and loving Providence. Only when these different values are given each their due importance, and only on the basis of the subordination of the physical to the moral, and the carnal to the spiritual can such excesses and laxity in marital relations as our decadent age is so sadly witnessing be avoided, and family life be restored to its original purity, and fulfill the true function for which it has been instituted by God.

"The Guardian will most fervently pray that, inspired and guided by such divine standard, and strengthened by Bahá'u'lláh's unfailing assistance and confirmations, you may be able to satisfactorily adjust your relations with the persons concerned, and thus reach the one right solution for this assuredly challenging problem of your life."

(Shoghi Effendi, from a letter dated May 8, 1939, written on his behalf
to a believer who, having married his first wife out of compassion, now wished
to be permitted to marry a woman with whom he had fallen in love,
saying that his wife was agreeable to his taking this second wife.)

30. "Regarding divorce, the Guardian stated that it is discouraged, deprecated and against the good pleasure of God. The Assembly must circulate among the friends whatever has been revealed from the Pen of 'Abdu'l-Bahá in this connection so that all may be fully reminded. Divorce is conditional upon the approval and permission of the Spiritual Assembly. The members of the Assembly must in such matters independently and carefully study and investigate each case. If there should be valid grounds for divorce and it is found that reconciliation is utterly impossible, that antipathy is intense and its removal is not possible, then the Assembly may approve the divorce."

(Shoghi Effendi, from a letter dated July 7, 1938,
to the National Spiritual Assembly of Iran)

31. "Shoghi Effendi wishes me to add this note in connection with your marriage; he does not feel that any believer, under any circum-

stances whatsoever, can ever use the Cause or service to it as a reason for abandoning their marriage; divorce, as we know it, is very strongly condemned by Bahá'u'lláh, and only grounds of extreme gravity justify it."

(Shoghi Effendi, from a letter dated April 7, 1947,
written on his behalf to an individual believer)

32. "Wherever there is a Bahá'í family, those concerned should by all means do all they can to preserve it, because divorce is strongly condemned in the Teachings, whereas harmony, unity and love are held up as the highest ideals in human relationships. This must always apply to the Bahá'ís, whether they are serving in the pioneering field or not."

(Shoghi Effendi, from a letter dated November 9, 1956,
written on his behalf to the National Spiritual Assembly of Central America)

33. "He wishes me to tell you that he regrets extremely the sorrow that has come into your life, and that he agrees with all you have stated in general on the subject of divorce.

"There is no doubt about it that the believers in America, probably unconsciously influenced by the extremely lax morals prevalent and the flippant attitude towards divorce which seems to be increasingly prevailing, do not take divorce seriously enough and do not seem to grasp the fact that although Bahá'u'lláh has permitted it, He has only permitted it as a last resort and *strongly condemns* it.

"The presence of children, as a factor in divorce, cannot be ignored, for surely it places an even greater weight of moral responsibility on the man and wife in considering such a step. Divorce under such circumstances no longer just concerns them and their desires and feelings but also concerns the children's entire future and their own attitude towards marriage."

(Shoghi Effendi, from a letter dated December 19, 1947,
written on his behalf to an individual believer)

34. "Divorce should be avoided most *strictly* by the believers, and only under rare and urgent circumstances be resorted to. Modern society is criminally lax as to the sacred nature of marriage, and the believers must combat this trend assiduously."

(Shoghi Effendi, from a letter dated January 5, 1948,
written on his behalf to an individual believer)

**35.** "He was very sorry to hear that you are contemplating separation from your husband. As you no doubt know, Bahá'u'lláh considers the marriage bond very sacred; and only under very exceptional and unbearable circumstances is divorce advisable for Bahá'ís.

"The Guardian does not tell you that you must not divorce your husband; but he does urge you to consider prayerfully, not only because you are a believer and anxious to obey the laws of God, but also for the sake of the happiness of your children, whether it is not possible for you to rise above the limitations you have felt in your marriage hitherto, and make a go of it together.

"We often feel that our happiness lies in a certain direction; and yet, if we have to pay too heavy a price for it in the end we may discover that we have not really purchased either freedom or happiness, but just some new situation of frustration and disillusion."

(Shoghi Effendi, from a letter dated April 5, 1951, written on his behalf to an individual believer)

**36.** "He was very sorry to hear that you and your husband are still so unhappy together. It is always a source of sorrow in life when married people cannot get on well together, but the Guardian feels that you and your husband, in contemplating divorce, should think of the future of your children and how this major step on your part will influence their lives and happiness.

"If you feel the need of advice and consultation he suggests you consult your local Assembly; your fellow Bahá'ís will surely do all they can to counsel and help you, protect your interests and those of the Cause."

(Shoghi Effendi, from a letter dated November 16, 1945, written on his behalf to an individual believer)

**37.** "Marriage is, in the Aqdas, set forth as a most sacred and binding tie, and the Bahá'ís should realize that divorce is viewed as a last resort, to be avoided at all costs if possible and not to be lightly granted."

(Shoghi Effendi, from a letter dated October 17, 1944, written on his behalf to an individual believer)

## F. Sex in Marriage

38. "... Enter ye into wedlock, that after you another may arise in your stead. We, verily, have forbidden you lechery, and not that which is conducive to fidelity ..."

(Bahá'u'lláh, *Epistle to the Son of the Wolf*, p. 49)

39. "'Enter into wedlock, O people, that ye may bring forth one who will make mention of Me amid My servants. This is my bidding unto you; hold fast to it as an assistance to yourselves.'"

(Bahá'u'lláh, *Bahá'í Prayers*, U.S. 1982, p. 105)

40. "Wherefore, wed Thou in the heaven of Thy mercy these two birds of the nest of Thy love, and make them the means of attracting perpetual grace: that from the union of these two seas of love a wave of tenderness may surge and cast the pearls of pure and goodly issue on the shore of life."

('Abdu'l-Bahá, *Bahá'í Prayers*, U.S. 1982, p. 188)

41. "Bahá'u'lláh has urged marriage upon all people as the natural and rightful way of life. He has also, however, placed strong emphasis on its spiritual nature, which, while in no way precluding a normal physical way of life, is the most essential aspect of marriage. That two people should live their lives in love and harmony is of far greater importance than that they should be consumed with passion for each other. The one is a great rock of strength on which to lean in time of need; the other is a purely temporary thing which may at any time die out."

(Shoghi Effendi, from a letter dated January 20, 1943, written on his behalf to an individual believer)

42. "The Bahá'í Faith recognizes the value of the sex impulse, but condemns its illegitimate and improper expressions such as free love, companionate marriage and others, all of which it considers positively harmful to man and to the society in which he lives. The proper use of the sex instinct is the natural right of every individual, and it is precisely for this very purpose that the institution of marriage has been estab-

lished. The Bahá'ís do not believe in the suppression of the sex impulse but in its regulation and control."

(Shoghi Effendi, from a letter dated September 5, 1938,
written on his behalf to an individual believer)

**43.** "The question you raise as to the place in one's life that a deep bond of love with someone we meet other than our husband or wife can have is easily defined in view of the teachings. Chastity implies both before and after marriage an unsullied, chaste sex life. Before marriage absolutely chaste, after marriage absolutely faithful to one's chosen companion. Faithful in all sexual acts, faithful in word and in deed.

"The world today is submerged, amongst other things, in an over-exaggeration of the importance of physical love, and a dearth of spiritual values. In as far as possible the believers should try to realize this and rise above the level of their fellow-men who are, typical of all decadent periods in history, placing so much over-emphasis on the purely physical side of mating. Outside of their normal, legitimate married life they should seek to establish bonds of comradeship and love which are eternal and founded on the spiritual life of man, not on his physical life. This is one of the many fields in which it is incumbent on the Bahá'ís to set the example and lead the way to a true human standard of life, when the soul of man is exalted and his body but the tool for his enlightened spirit. Needless to say this does not preclude the living of a perfectly normal sex life in its legitimate channel of marriage."

(Shoghi Effendi, from a letter dated September 28, 1941,
written on his behalf to an individual believer)

# II. PREPARATION FOR MARRIAGE

## A. Self-Knowledge

**44.** "O My servants! Could ye apprehend with what wonders of My munificence and bounty I have willed to entrust your souls, ye would, of a truth, rid yourselves of attachment to all created things, and would gain a true knowledge of your own selves—a knowledge which is the same as the comprehension of Mine own Being. Ye would find yourselves independent of all else but Me, and would perceive, with your inner and outer eye, and as manifest as the revelation of My effulgent Name, the seas of My loving-kindness and bounty moving within you."

(Bahá'u'lláh, *Gleanings from the Writings of Bahá'u'lláh*, pp. 326–327)

**45.** "Far, far from Thy glory be what mortal man can affirm of Thee, or attribute unto Thee, or the praise with which he can glorify Thee! Whatever duty Thou hast prescribed unto Thy servants of extolling to the utmost Thy majesty and glory is but a token of Thy grace unto them, that they may be enabled to ascend unto the station conferred upon their own inmost being, the station of the knowledge of their own selves."

(Bahá'u'lláh, *Gleanings from the Writings of Bahá'u'lláh*, pp. 4–5)

46. ". . . man should know his own self, and recognize that which leadeth unto loftiness or lowliness, glory or abasement, wealth or poverty."

(Bahá'u'lláh, *Tablets of Bahá'u'lláh*, p. 35)

## B. Choosing a Marriage Partner

47. "O SON OF SPIRIT!

"I created thee rich, why dost thou bring thyself down to poverty? Noble I made thee, wherewith dost thou abase thyself? Out of the essence of knowledge I gave thee being, why seekest thou enlightenment from anyone beside Me? Out of the clay of love I molded thee, how dost thou busy thyself with another? Turn thy sight unto thyself, that thou mayest find Me standing within thee, mighty, powerful and self-subsisting."

(Bahá'u'lláh, *The Hidden Words*, pp. 6–7)

48. "Disencumber yourselves of all attachment to this world and the vanities thereof. Beware that ye approach them not, inasmuch as they prompt you to walk after your own lusts and covetous desires, and hinder you from entering the straight and glorious Path."

(Bahá'u'lláh, *Gleanings from the Writings of Bahá'u'lláh*, p. 276)

49. "O SON OF BEING!

"Bring thyself to account each day ere thou art summoned to a reckoning; for death, unheralded, shall come upon thee and thou shalt be called to give account for thy deeds."

(Bahá'u'lláh, *The Hidden Words*, p. 11)

**50.** "O MY SON!"

"The company of the ungodly increaseth sorrow, whilst fellow-ship with the righteous cleanseth the rust from off the heart. He that seeketh to commune with God, let him betake himself to the companionship of His loved ones; and he that desireth to hearken to the word of God, let him give ear to the words of His chosen ones."

(Bahá'u'lláh, *The Hidden Words*, p. 42)

**51.** "Consultation bestoweth greater awareness and transmuteth conjecture into certitude. It is a shining light which, in a dark world, leadeth the way and guideth. For everything there is and will continue to be a station of perfection and maturity. The maturity of the gift of understanding is made manifest through consultation."

(Bahá'u'lláh, quoted in *Consultation: A Compilation*, no. 3)

**52.** "Now speak forth with fairness. Do not misrepresent the matter, neither to thyself nor to the people."

('Abdu'l-Bahá, *Tablets of Abdul-Baha Abbas*, Vol. I, p. 43)

**53.** "As for the question regarding marriage under the Law of God: first thou must choose one who is pleasing to thee, and then the matter is subject to the consent of father and mother. Before thou makest thy choice, they have no right to interfere."

('Abdu'l-Bahá, *Selections from the Writings of 'Abdu'l-Bahá*, 85.1)

**54.** "The love which exists between the hearts of believers is prompted by the ideal of the unity of spirits. This love is attained through the knowledge of God, so that men see the Divine Love reflected in the heart. Each sees in the other the Beauty of God reflected in the soul, and finding this point of similarity, they are attracted to one another in love. This love will make all men the waves of one sea, this love will make them all the stars of one heaven and the fruits of one tree. This love will bring the realization of true accord, the foundation of real unity.

"But the love which sometimes exists between friends is not (true) love, because it is subject to transmutation; this is merely fascination. As the breeze blows, the slender trees yield. If the wind is in the East the tree leans to the West, and if the wind turns to the West the tree leans to the East. This kind of love is originated by the accidental conditions of life. This is not love, it is merely acquaintanceship; it is subject to change.

"Today you will see two souls apparently in close friendship; tomorrow all this may be changed. Yesterday they were ready to die for one another, today they shun one another's society! This is not love; it is the yielding of the hearts to the accidents of life. When that which has caused this 'love' to exist passes, the love passes also; this is not in reality love."

('Abdu'l-Bahá, Paris Talks, 59.7–9)

**55.** "O thou son of the Kingdom! If one possesses the love of God, everything that he undertakes is useful, but if the undertaking is without the love of God, then it is hurtful and the cause of veiling one's self from the Lord of the Kingdom. But with the love of God every bitterness is changed into sweetness and every gift becometh precious. For instance, a musical and melodious voice imparteth life to an attracted heart but lureth toward lust those souls who are engulfed in passion and desire."

('Abdu'l-Bahá, quoted in Bahá'í World Faith, p. 366)

**56.** "It is extremely difficult to teach the individual and refine his character once puberty is passed. By then, as experience hath shown, even if every effort be exerted to modify some tendency of his, it all availeth nothing. He may, perhaps, improve somewhat today; but let a few days pass and he forgetteth, and turneth backward to his habitual condition and accustomed ways."

('Abdu'l-Bahá, Selections from the Writings of 'Abdu'l-Bahá, 111.7)

**57.** "But thou must submit to and rely upon God under all conditions and He will bestow upon thee that which is conducive to thy wellbeing. Verily He is the merciful and compassionate! For how many an affair was involved in difficulty and then was straightened, and how many a problem was solved by the permission of God."

('Abdu'l-Bahá, Tablets of Abdul-Baha Abbas, Vol. I, p. 10)

**58.** "If it be possible, gather together these two races, black and white, into one Assembly, and put such love into their hearts that they shall not only unite but even intermarry. Be sure that the result of this will abolish differences and disputes between black and white."

('Abdu'l-Bahá, quoted in *Bahá'í World Faith*, p. 359)

**59.** ". . . we must reach a spiritual plane where God comes first and great human passions are unable to turn us away from Him. All the time we see people who either through the force of hate or the passionate attachment they have to another person, sacrifice principle or bar themselves from the Path of God . . .

"We must love God, and in this state, a general love for all men becomes possible. We cannot love each human being for himself, but our feeling towards humanity should be motivated by our love for the Father who created all men."

(Shoghi Effendi, from a letter dated October 4, 1950, written on his behalf to an individual believer)

**60.** ". . . your statement to the effect that the principle of the oneness of mankind prevents any true Bahá'í from regarding race itself as a bar to union is in complete accord with the Teachings of the Faith on this point. For both Bahá'u'lláh and 'Abdu'l-Bahá never disapproved the idea of inter-racial marriage, nor discouraged it. The Bahá'í Teachings, indeed, by their very nature transcend all limitations imposed by race, and as such can and should never be identified with any particular school of racial philosophy."

(Shoghi Effendi, from a letter dated January 27, 1935, written on his behalf to the National Spiritual Assembly of the United States and Canada—*Bahá'í News*, no. 90, March 1935, p. 1)

**61.** "There is a difference between character and faith; it is often very hard to accept this fact and put up with it, but the fact remains that a person may believe in and love the Cause—even to being ready to die for it—and yet not have a good personal character, or possess traits at variance with the teachings. We should try to change, to let the Power of God help recreate us and make us true Bahá'ís in deed as well as in belief. But sometimes the process is slow, sometimes it never happens because the individual does not try hard enough. But these things cause us suffering and are a test to us . . ."

(Shoghi Effendi, from a letter dated October 17, 1944, written on his behalf to an individual believer)

**62.** "A couple should study each other's character and spend time getting to know each other before they decide to marry, and when they do marry it should be with the intention of establishing an eternal bond."

(Universal House of Justice, from a letter dated November 2, 1982, to an individual believer)

## C. Chastity

**63.** "We, verily, have decreed in Our Book a goodly and bountiful reward to whosoever will turn away from wickedness and lead a chaste and godly life. He, in truth, is the Great Giver, the All-Bountiful."

(Bahá'u'lláh, *Gleanings from the Writings of Bahá'u'lláh*, p. 117)

**64.** "I implore Thee, O Thou Fashioner of the nations and the King of eternity, to guard Thy handmaidens within the tabernacle of Thy chastity, and to cancel such of their deeds as are unworthy of Thy days."

(Bahá'u'lláh, *Prayers and Meditations*, p. 231)

**65.** "Purity and chastity have been, and still are, the most great ornaments for the handmaidens of God. God is My Witness! The brightness of the light of chastity sheddeth its illumination upon the worlds of the spirit, and its fragrance is wafted even unto the Most Exalted Paradise. God hath verily made chastity to be a crown for the heads of His handmaidens. Great is the blessedness of that handmaiden that hath attained unto this great station."

(Bahá'u'lláh, quoted in *The Advent of Divine Justice*, p. 27)

**66.** "Say: He is not to be numbered with the people of Bahá who followeth his mundane desires, or fixeth his heart on things of the earth ... if he met the fairest and most comely of women, he would not feel his heart seduced by the least shadow of desire for her beauty. Such an one, indeed, is the creation of spotless chastity. Thus instructeth you the Pen of the Ancient of Days, as bidden by your Lord, the Almighty, the All-Bountiful."

(Bahá'u'lláh, *Gleanings from the Writings of Bahá'u'lláh*, p. 118)

**67.** "As this physical frame is the throne of the inner temple, whatever occurs to the former is felt by the latter. In reality that which takes delight in joy or is saddened by pain is the inner temple of the body, not the body itself. Since this physical body is the throne whereon the inner temple is established, God hath ordained that the body be preserved to the extent possible, so that nothing that causeth repugnance may be experienced."

(The Báb, *Selections from the Writings of the Báb*, p. 95)

**68.** "Such a chaste and holy life, with its implications of modesty, purity, temperance, decency, and clean-mindedness, involves no less than the exercise of moderation in all that pertains to dress, language, amusements, and all artistic and literary avocations. It demands daily vigilance in the control of one's carnal desires and corrupt inclinations. It calls for the abandonment of a frivolous conduct, with its excessive attachment to trivial and often misdirected pleasures. It requires total abstinence from all alcoholic drinks, from opium, and from similar habit-forming drugs. It condemns the prostitution of art and literature, the practices of nudism and of companionate marriage, infidelity in marital relationships, and all manner of promiscuity, of easy familiarity, and of sexual vices. It can tolerate no compromise with the theories, the standards, the habits, and the excesses of a decadent age. Nay rather it seeks to demonstrate, through the dynamic force of its example, the pernicious character of such theories, the falsity of such standards, the hollowness of such claims, the perversity of such habits, and the sacrilegious character of such excesses."

(Shoghi Effendi, *The Advent of Divine Justice*, p. 25)

69. "Concerning your question whether there are any legitimate forms of expression of the sex instinct outside of marriage; according to the Bahá'í Teachings no sexual act can be considered lawful unless performed between lawfully married persons. Outside of marital life there can be no lawful or healthy use of the sex impulse. The Bahá'í youth should, on the one hand, be taught the lesson of self-control which, when exercised, undoubtedly has a salutary effect on the development of character and of personality in general, and on the other should be advised, nay even encouraged, to contract marriage while still young and in full possession of their physical vigor. Economic factors, no doubt, are often a serious hindrance to early marriage but in most cases are only an excuse, and as such should not be over stressed."

(Shoghi Effendi, from a letter dated December 13, 1940,
to an individual believer)

## D. Parental Consent

70. "Verily in the Book of Bayan (the Báb's Revelation) the matter is restricted to the consent of both (bride and bridegroom). As we desired to bring about love and friendship and the unity of the people, therefore We made it conditional upon the consent of the parents also, that enmity and ill-feeling might be avoided."

(Bahá'u'lláh, quoted in *Bahá'u'lláh and the New Era,* p. 182)

71. "Marriage is conditioned on the consent of both parties and their parents, whether the woman be a maiden or not."

(*Synopsis and Codification of the Laws and Ordinances
of the Kitáb-i-Aqdas,* p. 39)

72. "Bahá'u'lláh has clearly stated the consent of all living parents is required for Bahá'í marriage. This applies whether the parents are Bahá'ís or non-Bahá'ís, divorced for years or not. This great law He has laid down to strengthen the social fabric, to knit closer the ties of the home, to place a certain gratitude and respect in the hearts of children for those who have given them life and sent their souls out on the eternal

journey towards their Creator. We Bahá'ís must realize that in present-day society the exact opposite process is taking place: young people care less and less for their parents' wishes, divorce is considered a natural right, and obtained on the flimsiest and most unwarrantable and shabby pretexts. People separated from each other, especially if one of them has had full custody of the children, are only too willing to belittle the importance of the partner in marriage also responsible as a parent for bringing those children into this world. The Bahá'ís must, through rigid adherence to the Bahá'í laws and teachings, combat these corrosive forces which are so rapidly destroying home life and the beauty of family relationships, and tearing down the moral structure of society."

(Shoghi Effendi, from a letter dated October 25, 1947, written on his behalf
to the National Spiritual Assembly of the United States)

73. "The validity of a Bahá'í marriage is dependent upon the free and full consent of all four parents. The freedom of the parents in the exercise of this right is unrestricted and unconditioned. They may refuse their consent on any ground, and they are responsible for their decision to God alone."

(Shoghi Effendi, from a letter dated March 19, 1938,
written on his behalf to an individual believer)

74. "It is surely a very unfortunate case when the parents and children differ on some grave issues of life such as marriage, but the best way is not to flout each other's opinion nor to discuss it in a charged atmosphere but rather try to settle it in an amicable way."

(Shoghi Effendi, from a letter dated May 29, 1929,
written on his behalf to an individual believer)

75. "I notice that I have neglected to answer your question concerning . . . consent to her daughter's marriage: this must be given in order to be a Bahá'í Marriage. Bahá'u'lláh requires this and makes no provision about a parent changing his or her mind. So they are free to do so. Once the written consent is given and the marriage takes place, the parents have no right to interfere any more."

(Shoghi Effendi, *Messages to Canada*, p. 47)

**76.** "We gain the impression from Mr. . . .'s letter that he looks upon the law requiring consent of parents before marriage as a mere administrative regulation, and does not realize that this is a law of great importance affecting the very foundations of human society. Moreover, he seems not to appreciate that in the Bahá'í Faith the spiritual and administrative aspects are complementary and that the social laws of the Faith are as binding as the purely spiritual ones."

(Universal House of Justice, from a letter dated December 4, 1964,
to the National Spiritual Assembly of North East Asia)

**77.** "It is perfectly true that Bahá'u'lláh's statement that the consent of all living parents is required for marriage places a grave responsibility on each parent. When the parents are Bahá'ís they should, of course act objectively in withholding or granting their approval. They cannot evade this responsibility by merely acquiescing in their child's wish, nor should they be swayed by prejudice; but, whether they be Bahá'í or non-Bahá'í, the parents' decision is binding, whatever the reason that may have motivated it. Children must recognize and understand that this act of consenting is the duty of a parent. They must have respect in their hearts for those who have given them life, and whose good pleasure they must at all times strive to win."

(Universal House of Justice, from a letter dated February 1, 1968,
to the National Spiritual Assembly of the United States)

**78.** ". . . consent of parents must be obtained in all cases before marriage can take place. Obedience to the laws of Bahá'u'lláh will necessarily impose hardships in individual cases. No one should expect, upon becoming a Bahá'í, that his faith will not be tested, and to our finite understanding of such matters these tests may occasionally seem unbearable. But we are aware of the assurance which Bahá'u'lláh Himself has given the believers that they will never be called upon to meet a test greater than their capacity to endure."

(Universal House of Justice, from a letter dated January 29, 1970,
to the National Spiritual Assembly of the Hawaiian Islands)

**79.** ". . . Foster parents or relatives who may act in loco parentis are not required by Bahá'í law to give their consent to the marriage of the children they raise although there is no objection to the children obtaining such consent, should they wish to do so."

(Universal House of Justice, from a letter dated April 9, 1970, to the National Spiritual Assembly of Italy)

**80.** "Bahá'ís who cannot marry because of lack of consent of one or more parents could consult with their Local Spiritual Assembly, to see whether it may suggest a way to change the attitude of any of the parents involved. The believers, when faced with such problems, should put their trust in Bahá'u'lláh, devote more time to the service, the teaching and the promotion of His Faith, be absolutely faithful to His injunctions on the observance of an unsullied, chaste life, and rely upon Him to open the way and remove the obstacle, or make known His will."

(Universal House of Justice, from a letter dated September 9, 1969, to an individual believer)

**81.** "In considering the effect of obedience to the laws on individual lives, one must remember that the purpose of this life is to prepare the soul for the next. Here one must learn to control and direct one's animal impulses, not to be a slave to them. Life in this world is a succession of tests and achievements, of falling short and of making new spiritual advances. Sometimes the course may seem very hard, but one can witness, again and again, that the soul who steadfastly obeys the law of Bahá'u'lláh, however hard it may seem, grows spiritually, while the one who compromises with the law for the sake of his own apparent happiness is seen to have been following a chimera: he does not attain the happiness he sought, he retards his spiritual advance and often brings new problems upon himself.

"To give one very obvious example: The Bahá'í law requiring consent of parents to marriage. All too often nowadays such consent is withheld by non-Bahá'í parents for reasons of bigotry or racial prejudice; yet we have seen again and again the profound effect on those very parents of the firmness of the children in the Bahá'í law, to the extent that not only is the consent ultimately given in many cases, but the character of the parents can be affected and their relationship with their child greatly strengthened.

"Thus, by upholding Bahá'í law in the face of all difficulties we not only strengthen our own characters but influence those around us."

(Universal House of Justice, *Messages from the Universal House of Justice, 1963–1986*, 126.4–6)

## E. Engagement

82. "Concerning the question of marriage and the stipulated period between the time of the engagement and the marriage, this is the decisive text of the Book of God and may not be interpreted. In the past, serious difficulties and problems arose when a long period of time elapsed between the engagement and the marriage. Now according to the Text of the Book, when marriage between the parties is arranged, i.e. when the parties become engaged, and it is certain that they will be married, not more than ninety-five days should elapse before the marriage takes place . . ."

('Abdu'l-Bahá, quoted in a letter dated April 11, 1982, from the Universal House of Justice to the National Spiritual Assembly of the United States)

83. "The beginning of the ninety-five days before the marriage is the day on which the consents have been obtained."

(Shoghi Effendi, from a letter dated April 3, 1943, to an individual believer)

84. "The law requiring Bahá'ís to be married within the ninety-five day period following the engagement is not yet applicable in the West. However, Iranians residing in the West obey such laws as a matter of conscience."

(Universal House of Justice, from a letter dated July 14, 1965, to a National Spiritual Assembly)

**85.** "Concerning the observance of details of Bahá'í law pertaining to marriage such as the duration of the engagement period . . . by the Iranian believers now residing in the West, these laws are binding if the two parties are Iranians. However, if one party is Iranian and the other is a western believer, the Iranian believer, although it is a praiseworthy act to inform his/her spouse of these laws, should not bring pressure to bear for their observance."

(Universal House of Justice, from a letter dated
July 7, 1968, to an individual believer)

# III. FAMILY LIFE

## A. Love and Unity

**86.** "At all times hath union and association been well-pleasing in the sight of God, and separation and dissension abhorred. Hold fast unto that which God loveth and is His command unto you. He, verily, is the All-Knowing and the All-Seeing, and He is the All-Wise Ordainer."

(Bahá'u'lláh, quoted in a compilation dated January 18, 1980, sent by the
Universal House of Justice to National Spiritual Assemblies)

**87.** "After man's recognition of God, and becoming steadfast in His Cause the station of affection, of harmony, of concord and of unity is superior to that of most other goodly deeds. This is what He Who is the Desire of the world hath testified at every morn and eve. God grant that ye may follow that which hath been revealed in the Kitáb-i-Aqdas."

(Bahá'u'lláh, quoted in a compilation dated January 18, 1980, sent by the
Universal House of Justice to National Spiritual Assemblies)

**88.** "Deal ye one with another with the utmost love and harmony, with friendliness and fellowship. He Who is the Day Star of Truth beareth Me witness! So powerful is the light of unity that it can illuminate the whole earth. The one true God, He Who knoweth all things, Himself testifieth to the truth of these words."

(Bahá'u'lláh, *Gleanings from the Writings of Bahá'u'lláh*, p. 288)

**89.** "The advent of the prophets and the revelation of the Holy Books is intended to create love between souls and friendship between the inhabitants of the earth. Real love is impossible unless one turn his face towards God and be attracted to His Beauty."

('Abdu'l-Bahá, quoted in *Bahá'í World Faith*, p. 364)

**90.** "The great and fundamental teachings of Bahá'u'lláh are the oneness of God and unity of mankind. This is the bond of union among Bahá'ís all over the world. They become united themselves, then unite others. It is impossible to unite unless united."

('Abdu'l-Bahá, *The Promulgation of Universal Peace*, p. 156)

**91.** "When you love a member of your family or a compatriot, let it be with a ray of the Infinite Love! Let it be in God, and for God! Wherever you find the attributes of God love that person, whether he be of your family or of another. Shed the light of a boundless love on every human being whom you meet . . ."

('Abdu'l-Bahá, *Paris Talks*, 9.21)

**92.** "Compare the nations of the world to the members of a family. A family is a nation in miniature. Simply enlarge the circle of the household and you have the nation. Enlarge the circle of nations and you have all humanity. The conditions surrounding the family surround the nation. The happenings in the family are the happenings in the life of the nation. Would it add to the progress and advancement of a family if dissensions should arise among its members, fighting, pillaging each other, jealous and revengeful of injury, seeking selfish advantage? Nay, this would be the cause of the effacement of progress and advancement. So it is in the great family of nations, for nations are but an aggregate of families."

('Abdu'l-Bahá, *The Promulgation of Universal Peace*, p. 157)

**93.** "It is highly important for man to raise a family. So long as he is young, because of youthful self-complacency, he does not realize its significance, but this will be a source of regret when he grows old. . . . In this glorious Cause the life of a married couple should resemble the life of the angels in heaven—a life full of joy and spiritual delight, a life of unity and concord, a friendship both mental and physical. The home should be orderly and well-organized. Their ideas and thoughts should be like the rays of the sun of truth and the radiance of the brilliant stars in the heavens. Even as two birds they should warble melodies upon the branches of the tree of fellowship and harmony. They should always be elated with joy and gladness and be a source of happiness to the hearts of others. They should set an example to their fellow-men, manifest true and sincere love towards each other and educate their children in such a manner as to blazon the fame and glory of their family."

('Abdu'l-Bahá, quoted in a compilation on Family Life dated January 1982 sent by the Universal House of Justice to National Spiritual Assemblies)

**94.** "Consider the harmful effect of discord and dissension in a family; then reflect upon the favors and blessings which descend upon that family when unity exists among its various members. What incalculable benefits and blessings would descend upon the great human family if unity and brotherhood were established! In this century when the beneficent results of unity and the ill effects of discord are so clearly apparent, the means for the attainment and accomplishment of human fellowship have appeared in the world. His Holiness Bahá'u'lláh has proclaimed and provided the way by which hostility and dissension may be removed from the human world. He has left no ground or possibility for strife and disagreement. First he has proclaimed the oneness of mankind and specialized religious teachings for existing human conditions."

('Abdu'l-Bahá, quoted in *Star of the West*, Vol. XVII, No. 7, p. 232)

**95.** "Note ye how easily, where unity existeth in a given family, the affairs of that family are conducted; what progress the members of that family make, how they prosper in the world. Their concerns are in order, they enjoy comfort and tranquillity, they are secure, their position is assured, they come to be envied by all. Such a family but addeth to its stature and its lasting honor, as day succeedeth day."

('Abdu'l-Bahá, *Selections from the Writings of 'Abdu'l-Bahá*, 221.9)

**96.** "If love and agreement are manifest in a single family, that family will advance, become illumined and spiritual; but if enmity and hatred exist within it, destruction and dispersion are inevitable."

('Abdu'l-Bahá, *The Promulgation of Universal Peace*, pp. 144–145)

**97.** "I charge you all that each one of you concentrate all the thoughts of your heart on love and unity . . .

"Thoughts of love are constructive of brotherhood, peace, friendship, and happiness."

('Abdu'l-Bahá, *Paris Talks*, 6.7, 8)

**98.** "Know thou of a certainty that Love is the secret of God's holy Dispensation, the manifestation of the All-Merciful, the fountain of spiritual outpourings. Love is heaven's kindly light, the Holy Spirit's eternal breath that vivifies the human soul. Love is the cause of God's revelation unto man, the vital bond inherent, according to Divine creation, in the realities of things. Love is the one means that insures true felicity both in this world and the next. Love is the light that guideth in darkness, the living link that united God with man, that assureth the progress of every illumined soul."

('Abdu'l-Bahá, quoted in *The Bahá'í World*, Vol. II, p. 50)

**99.** ". . . human evolution . . . had its earliest beginnings in the birth of family life, its subsequent development in the achievement of tribal solidarity, leading in turn to the constitution of the city-state, and expanding later into the institution of independent and sovereign nations."

(Shoghi Effendi, *The World Order of Bahá'u'lláh*, p. 43)

**100.** ". . . the Cause has not come to break up family ties but to strengthen them; it has not come to eliminate love but to strengthen it; it has not been created to weaken social institutions but to strengthen them."

(Shoghi Effendi, from a letter dated October 14, 1928,<br>written on his behalf to an individual believer)

**101.** "If we Bahá'ís cannot attain to cordial unity among ourselves, then we fail to realize the main purpose for which the Báb, Bahá'u'lláh, and the Beloved Master lived and suffered.

"In order to achieve this cordial unity, one of the first essentials insisted on by Bahá'u'lláh and 'Abdu'l-Bahá is that we resist the natural tendency to let our attention dwell on the faults and failings of others rather than on our own. Each of us is responsible for one life only, and that is our own. Each of us is immeasurably far from being 'perfect as our heavenly Father is perfect' and the task of perfecting our own life and character is one that requires all our attention, our will-power and energy. If we allow our attention and energy to be taken up in efforts to keep others right and remedy their faults, we are wasting precious time. We are like ploughmen each of whom has his team to manage and his plough to direct, and in order to keep his furrow straight he must keep his eye on his goal and concentrate on his own task. If he looks to this side and that to see how Tom and Harry are getting on and to criticize their ploughing, then his own furrow will assuredly become crooked.

"On no subject are the Bahá'í teachings more emphatic than on the necessity to abstain from fault-finding and backbiting while being ever eager to discover and root out our own faults and overcome our own failings.

"If we profess loyalty to Bahá'u'lláh, to our Beloved Master and our dear Guardian, then we must show our love by obedience to these explicit teachings. Deeds not words are what they demand, and no amount of fervor in the use of expressions of loyalty and adulation will compensate for failure to live in the spirit of the teachings."

(Shoghi Effendi, from a letter dated May 12, 1925,<br>written on his behalf to an individual believer)

## B. Communication

**102.** "If ye be aware of a certain truth, if ye possess a jewel, of which others are deprived, share it with them in a language of utmost kindliness and good-will. If it be accepted, if it fulfill its purpose, your object is attained. If any one should refuse it, leave him unto himself, and beseech God to guide him. Beware lest ye deal unkindly with him. A kindly tongue is the lodestone of the hearts of men. It is the bread of the spirit, it clotheth the words with meaning, it is the fountain of the light of wisdom and understanding . . ."

(Bahá'u'lláh, *Gleanings from the Writings of Bahá'u'lláh*, p. 289)

**103.** "The Great Being saith: The heaven of divine wisdom is illumined with the two luminaries of consultation and compassion. Take ye counsel together in all matters, inasmuch as consultation is the lamp of guidance which leadeth the way, and is the bestower of understanding."

(Bahá'u'lláh, quoted in *Consultation: A Compilation,* no. 1)

**104.** "Say: no man can attain his true station except through his justice. No power can exist except through unity. No welfare and no well-being can be attained except through consultation."

(Bahá'u'lláh, quoted in *Consultation: A Compilation,* no. 2)

**105.** "Consultation bestoweth greater awareness and transmuteth conjecture into certitude. It is a shining light which, in a dark world, leadeth the way and guideth. For everything there is and will continue to be a station of perfection and maturity. The maturity of the gift of understanding is made manifest through consultation."

(Bahá'u'lláh, quoted in *Consultation: A Compilation,* no. 3)

**106.** "In all things it is necessary to consult. This matter should be forcibly stressed by thee, so that consultation may be observed by all. The intent of what hath been revealed from the Pen of the Most High is that consultation may be fully carried out among the friends, inasmuch as it is and will always be a cause of awareness and of awakening and a source of good and well-being."

(Bahá'u'lláh, quoted in Consultation: A Compilation, no. 5)

**107.** "Trust in God and be unmoved by either praise or false accusations . . . depend entirely on God."

('Abdu'l-Bahá, Tablets of Abdul-Baha Abbas, Vol. I, p. 158)

**108.** "Settle all things, both great and small, by consultation. Without prior consultation, take no important step in your own personal affairs. Concern yourselves with one another. Help along one another's projects and plans. Grieve over one another. Let none in the whole country go in need. Befriend one another until ye become as a single body, one and all . . ."

('Abdu'l-Bahá, quoted in Consultation: A Compilation, no. 19)

**109.** "The prime requisites for them that take counsel together are purity of motive, radiance of spirit, detachment from all else save God, attraction to His Divine Fragrances, humility and lowliness amongst His loved ones, patience and long-suffering in difficulties and servitude to His exalted Threshold. Should they be graciously aided to acquire these attributes, victory from the unseen Kingdom of Bahá shall be vouchsafed to them."

('Abdu'l-Bahá, Selections from the Writings of 'Abdu'l-Bahá, 43.1)

**110.** "The members thereof must take counsel together in such wise that no occasion for ill-feeling or discord may arise. This can be attained when every member expresseth with absolute freedom his own opinion and setteth forth his argument. Should anyone oppose, he must on no account feel hurt for not until matters are fully discussed can the right way be revealed. The shining spark of truth cometh forth only after the clash of differing opinions . . ."

('Abdu'l-Bahá, Selections from the Writings of 'Abdu'l-Bahá, 44.1)

**111.** "If they agree upon a subject, even though it be wrong, it is better than to disagree and be in the right, for this difference will produce the demolition of the divine foundation. Though one of the parties may be in the right and they disagree that will be the cause of a thousand wrongs, but if they agree and both parties are in the wrong, as it is in unity the truth will be revealed and the wrong made right."

(ʻAbduʼl-Bahá, quoted in *Bahá'í World Faith*, p. 411)

**112.** "According to the direct command of God we are forbidden to utter slander. Remember above all the teaching of Bahá'u'lláh concerning gossip and unseemly talk about others. Stories repeated about others are seldom good. A silent tongue is safest. Even good may be harmful if spoken at the wrong time or to the wrong person."

(ʻAbduʼl-Bahá, *ʻAbduʼl-Bahá in London*, p. 131)

**113.** "To be silent concerning the faults of others, to pray for them, and to help them, through kindness, to correct their faults.

"To look always at the good and not at the bad. If a man has ten good qualities and one bad one, to look at the ten and forget the one; and if a man has ten bad qualities and one good one, to look at the one and forget the ten.

"Never to allow ourselves to speak one unkind word about another, even though that other be our enemy."

(ʻAbduʼl-Bahá, quoted in *Bahá'u'lláh and the New Era*, p. 94)

**114.** "Man must consult on all matters, whether major or minor, so that he may become cognizant of what is good. Consultation giveth him insight into things and enableth him to delve into questions which are unknown. The light of truth shineth from the faces of those who engage in consultation. Such consultation causeth the living waters to flow in the meadows of man's reality, the rays of ancient glory to shine upon him, and the tree of his being to be adorned with wondrous fruit. The members who are consulting, however, should behave in the utmost love, harmony and sincerity towards each other. The principle of consultation is one of the most fundamental elements of the divine edifice. Even in their ordinary affairs the individual members of society should consult."

(ʻAbduʼl-Bahá, quoted in *Consultation: A Compilation*, no. 14)

**115.** "Bahá'u'lláh also stressed the importance of consultation. We should not think this worthwhile method of seeking solutions is confined to the administrative institutions of the Cause. Family consultation employing full and frank discussion, and animated by awareness of the need for moderation and balance, can be the panacea for domestic conflict."

(Universal House of Justice, from a letter dated
August 1, 1978, to an individual believer)

## C. Tests and Difficulties

**116.** "O SON OF MAN!

"My calamity is My providence, outwardly it is fire and vengeance, but inwardly it is light and mercy. Hasten thereunto that thou mayest become an eternal light and an immortal spirit. This is My command unto thee, do thou observe it."

(Bahá'u'lláh, *The Hidden Words*, p. 15)

**117.** "O BEFRIENDED STRANGER!

"The candle of thine heart is lighted by the hand of My power, quench it not with the contrary winds of self and passion. The healer of all thine ills is remembrance of me, forget it not. Make My love thy treasure and cherish it even as thy very sight and life."

(Bahá'u'lláh, *The Hidden Words*, p. 33)

**118.** "Verily the most necessary thing is contentment under all circumstances; by this one is preserved from morbid conditions and from lassitude. Yield not to grief and sorrow; they cause the greatest misery. Jealousy consumeth the body and anger doth burn the liver; avoid these two as you would a lion."

(Bahá'u'lláh, quoted in *Bahá'u'lláh and the New Era*, p. 117)

**119.** "If any differences arise amongst you, behold Me standing before your face, and overlook the faults of one another for My name's sake and as a token of your love for My manifest and resplendent Cause. We love to see you at all times consorting in amity and concord within the paradise of My good-pleasure, and to inhale from your acts the fragrance of friendliness and unity, of loving-kindness and fellowship."

(Bahá'u'lláh, *Gleanings from the Writings of Bahá'u'lláh*, p. 315)

120. "O thou who art firm in the Covenant! The letter thou hadst written on 2 May 1919 was received. Praise thou God that in tests thou art firm and steadfast and art holding fast to the Abhá Kingdom. Thou art not shaken by any affliction or disturbed by any calamity. Not until man is tried doth the pure gold distinctly separate from the dross. Torment is the fire of test wherein the pure gold shineth resplendently and the impurity is burned and blackened. At present thou art, praise be to God, firm and steadfast in tests and trials and art not shaken by them."

('Abdu'l-Bahá, *Selections from the Writings of 'Abdu'l-Bahá*, 89.1)

121. "Rely upon God. Trust in Him. Praise Him, and call Him continually to mind. He verily turneth trouble into ease, and sorrow into solace, and toil into utter peace. He verily hath dominion over all things."

('Abdu'l-Bahá, *Selections from the Writings of 'Abdu'l-Bahá*, 150.3)

122. "If thy daily living become difficult, soon (God) thy Lord will bestow upon thee that which will satisfy thee. Be patient in the time of affliction and trial, endure every difficulty and hardship with a dilated heart, attracted spirit and eloquent tongue in remembrance of the Merciful. Verily this is the life of satisfaction, the spiritual existence, heavenly repose, divine benediction and the celestial table! Soon thy Lord will extenuate thy straitened circumstances even in this world."

('Abdu'l-Bahá, *Tablets of Abdul-Baha Abbas*, Vol. I, p. 98)

123. "As to thy respected husband: it is incumbent upon thee to treat him with great kindness, to consider his wishes and be conciliatory with him at all times, till he seeth that because thou hast directed thyself toward the Kingdom of God, thy tenderness for him and thy love for

God have but increased, as well as thy concern for his wishes under all conditions."

('Abdu'l-Bahá, *Selections from the Writings of 'Abdu'l-Bahá*, 91.2)

**124.** "Thy wife is not in harmony with thee, but praise be to God, the Blessed Beauty is pleased with thee and is conferring upon thee the utmost bounty and blessings. But still try to be patient with thy wife, perchance she may be transformed and her heart may be illumined."

('Abdu'l-Bahá, *Selections from the Writings of 'Abdu'l-Bahá*, 89.2)

**125.** "We should not, however, forget that an essential characteristic of this world is hardship and tribulation and that it is by overcoming them that we achieve our moral and spiritual development. As the Master says, sorrow is like furrows, the deeper they go, the more plentiful is the fruit we obtain."

(Shoghi Effendi, from a letter dated November 5, 1931, written on his behalf to an individual believer)

**126.** "We must always look ahead and seek to accomplish in the future what we may have failed to do in the past. Failures, tests, and trials, if we use them correctly, can become the means of purifying our spirits, strengthening our characters, and enable us to rise to greater heights of service."

(Shoghi Effendi, from a letter dated December 14, 1941, written on his behalf to an individual believer)

**127.** "We must not only be patient with others, infinitely patient!, but also with our own poor selves, remembering that even the Prophets of God sometimes got tired and cried out in despair!"

(Shoghi Effendi, from a letter dated April 5, 1956, written on his behalf to an individual believer)

**128.** "He feels that you should by all means make every effort to hold your marriage together, especially for the sake of your children, who, like all children of divorced parents, cannot but suffer from conflicting loyalties, for they are deprived of the blessings of a father and mother in one home, to look after their interests and love them jointly.

"Now that you realize that your husband is ill, you should be able to reconcile yourself to the difficulties you have faced with him emotionally, and not take an unforgiving attitude, however much you may suffer.

"We know that Bahá'u'lláh has very strongly frowned on divorce; and it is really incumbent upon the Bahá'ís to make almost a superhuman effort not to allow a marriage to be dissolved."

(Shoghi Effendi, from a letter dated March 6, 1953,
written on his behalf to an individual believer)

**129.** "When such differences of opinion and belief occurs between husband and wife it is very unfortunate for undoubtedly it detracts from that spiritual bond which is the stronghold of the family bond, especially in times of difficulty. The way, however, that it could be remedied is not by acting in such wise as to alienate the other party. One of the objects of the Cause is actually to bring about a closer bond in the homes. In all such cases, therefore, the Master used to advise obedience to the wishes of the other party and prayer. Pray that your husband may gradually see the light and at the same time so act as to draw him nearer rather than prejudice him. Once that harmony is secured then you will be able to serve unhampered."

(Shoghi Effendi, from a letter dated July 15, 1928,
written on his behalf to an individual believer)

**130.** "He feels that, now that you have found the thing you were searching for inwardly, and have this added joy in your life of our glorious Faith, you should be kinder to your husband and more considerate than ever, and do everything in your power to make him feel that this has not taken you away from him, but only made your love for him, and your desire to be a good wife to him, greater. Whether he will ultimately be able to become a Bahá'í or not, is something that only time can tell; but there is no doubt where your duty lies, and that is to make him appreciate the fact that your new affiliation has not interfered in any way with his home life or his marriage, but, on the contrary, has strengthened both.

"It is very difficult when one has found what one knows is the truth, to sit by and see a dear and close relative completely blind to it. The temptation is to try and 'stir them up and make them see the light,' but this is often disastrous. Silence, love and forbearance will win greater victories in such cases. However, your husband has no right to ask you to give up being a Bahá'í. That is going too far. Nobody should trespass on the sacred bond every human being has a right to have with their Creator."

(Shoghi Effendi, from a letter dated April 20, 1957,
written on his behalf to an individual believer)

**131.** "The Guardian . . . has learned with deep concern of your family difficulties and troubles. He wishes me to assure you of his fervent prayers on your behalf and your dear ones at home, that you may be guided and assisted from on high to compose your differences and to restore complete harmony and fellowship in your midst. While he would urge you to make any sacrifice in order to bring about unity in your family, he wishes you not to feel discouraged if your endeavors do not yield any immediate fruit. You should do your part with absolute faith that in doing so you are fulfilling your duty as a Bahá'í. The rest is assuredly in God's hand.

"As regards your husband's attitude towards the Cause; unfriendly though that may be you should always hope that, through conciliatory and friendly means, and with wise, tactful and patient effort you can gradually succeed in winning his sympathy for the Faith. Under no circumstances should you try to dictate and impose upon him by force your personal religious convictions. Neither should you allow his opposition to the Cause to seriously hinder your activities . . . You should act patiently, tactfully and with confidence that your efforts are being guided and reinforced by Bahá'u'lláh."

(Shoghi Effendi, from a letter dated July 23, 1937,
written on his behalf to an individual believer)

**132.** "He was very sorry to see you are having trouble in your home because of the Bahá'í Faith. He feels that you should do all in your power to promote love and harmony between your husband and yourself, for your own sakes and for the sake of your children. You should,

however, point out to him that every man is free to seek God for himself, and that, although you will never seek to influence him or even discuss the Bahá'í Faith with him, if he does not want to, he should leave you free to attend the meetings. The Guardian hopes that through patience, tact and prayer, you will gradually overcome his prejudice."
(Shoghi Effendi, from a letter dated March 16, 1946, written on his behalf to an individual believer)

**133.** "The Guardian wishes me specially to urge you to remain patient and confident, and above all to show your husband the utmost kindness and love, in return for all the opposition and hatred you receive from him. A conciliatory and friendly attitude in such cases is not only the duty of every Bahá'í but is also the most effective way of winning for the Cause the sympathy and admiration of its former foes and enemies. Love is, indeed, a most potent elixir that can transform the vilest and meanest of people into heavenly souls. May your example serve to further confirm the truth of this beautiful teaching of our Faith."
(Shoghi Effendi, from a letter dated December 6, 1935, written on his behalf to an individual believer)

**134.** "However, as you no doubt know, Bahá'u'lláh has stated that the purpose of marriage is to promote unity, so you should bear this in mind when dealing with your non-Bahá'í relatives; they cannot be expected to feel the way we do on questions of racial amity, and we must not force our views on them, but rather lovingly and wisely seek to educate them."
(Shoghi Effendi, from a letter dated August 30, 1957, written on his behalf to an individual believer)

**135.** "There is no limit to our offerings to the Temple. The more we give, the better it is for the Cause and for ourselves. But your case is a special one, since your husband is not a believer. If you can succeed in convincing him of the importance of your donations to the Cause, so much the better. But you should never oppose him on this matter and allow anything to disturb the peace and unity of your family life."
(Shoghi Effendi from a letter dated September 21, 1933, written on his behalf to an individual believer)

**136.** "Regarding your other question concerning the strained relationship between you and your mother-in-law and what you can do to alleviate the situation, we feel you should, with the help and consultation of your husband, persevere in your efforts to achieve unity in the family. From your description of the unfriendly attitude your mother-in-law displays toward you it is clear that you will not have an easy task. However, the important thing is that you, as a Bahá'í, are aware of 'Abdu'l-Bahá's admonition to concentrate on an individual's good qualities and that this approach to your mother-in-law can strengthen you in your resolve to achieve unity. And furthermore, perseverance in prayer will give you the strength to continue your efforts."

(Universal House of Justice, from a letter dated
September 6, 1980, to an individual believer)

**137.** "The House of Justice points out that learning not to concern oneself with the faults of others seems to be one of the most difficult lessons for people to master, and that failing in this is a fertile cause of disputes among Bahá'ís as it is among men and women in general. In 'Star of the West,' Volume 8, No. 10, on page 138, there is a record of a reply given by 'Abdu'l-Bahá in a private interview in Paris in 1913. He was asked 'How shall I overcome seeing the faults of others—recognizing the wrong in others?' and He replied: 'I will tell you. Whenever you recognize the fault of another, think of yourself: What are my imperfections?—and try to remove them. Do this whenever you are tried through the words or deeds of others. Thus you will grow, become more perfect. You will overcome self, you will not even have time to think of the faults of others . . .'"

(Universal House of Justice, from a letter dated
April 5, 1981, written on its behalf to an individual believer)

**138.** "In considering the problems that you and your wife are experiencing, the House of Justice points out that the unity of your family should take priority over any other consideration . . . For example, service to the Cause should not produce neglect of the family. It is important for you to arrange your time so that your family life is harmonious and your household receives the attention it requires."

(Universal House of Justice, from a letter dated
August 1, 1978, to an individual believer)

## D. Equality of Men and Women

**139.** "O CHILDREN OF MEN!

"Know ye not why We created you all from the same dust? That no one should exalt himself over the other. Ponder at all times in your hearts how ye were created. Since We have created you all from one substance it is incumbent on you to be even as one soul, to walk with the same feet, eat with the same mouth and dwell in the same land, that from your inmost being, by your deeds and actions, the signs of oneness and the essence of detachment may be made manifest. Such is My counsel to you, O concourse of light! Heed ye this counsel that ye may obtain the fruit of holiness from the tree of wondrous glory."

(Bahá'u'lláh, *The Hidden Words*, p. 20)

**140.** "Humanity is like a bird with its two wings—the one is male, the other female. Unless both wings are strong and impelled by some common force, the bird cannot fly heavenwards. According to the spirit of this age, women must advance and fulfill their mission in all departments of life, becoming equal to men. They must be on the same level as men and enjoy equal rights. This is my earnest prayer and it is one of the fundamental principles of Bahá'u'lláh."

('Abdu'l-Bahá, quoted in *Bahá'u'lláh and the New Era*, p. 154)

**141.** "Divine justice demands that the rights of both sexes should be equally respected since neither is superior to the other in the eyes of Heaven. Dignity before God depends not on sex, but on purity and luminosity of heart. Human virtues belong equally to all!"

('Abdu'l-Bahá, *Paris Talks*, 50.10)

**142.** "Women have equal rights with men upon earth; in religion and society they are a very important element. As long as women are prevented from attaining their highest possibilities, so long will men be unable to achieve the greatness which might be theirs."

('Abdu'l-Bahá, *Paris Talks*, 40.33)

**143.** "In the world of humanity we find a great difference; the female sex is treated as though inferior, and is not allowed equal rights and privileges. This condition is due not to nature, but to education. In the Divine Creation there is no such distinction. Neither sex is superior to the other in the sight of God. Why then should one sex assert the inferiority of the other, withholding just rights and privileges as though God had given His authority for such a course of action? If women received the same educational advantages as those of men, the result would demonstrate the equality of capacity of both for scholarship."

('Abdu'l-Bahá, *Paris Talks*, 50.5)

144. "His Holiness Bahá'u'lláh has greatly strengthened the cause of women, and the rights and privileges of women is one of the greatest principles of 'Abdu'l-Bahá. Rest ye assured! Ere long the days shall come when the men addressing the women shall say: 'Blessed are ye! Blessed are ye! Verily ye are worthy of every gift. Verily ye deserve to adorn your heads with the crown of everlasting glory, because in sciences and arts, in virtues and perfections ye shall become equal to man, and as regards tenderness of heart and the abundance of mercy and sympathy ye are superior.'"

('Abdu'l-Bahá, *Paris Talks*, 59.8)

145. "In this Revelation of Bahá'u'lláh, the women go neck and neck with the men. In no movement will they be left behind. Their rights with men are equal in degree. They will enter all the administrative branches of politics. They will attain in all such a degree as will be considered the very highest station of the world of humanity and will take part in all affairs. Rest ye assured. Do ye not look upon the present conditions; in the not far distant future the world of women will become all-refulgent and all-glorious FOR HIS HOLINESS BAHÁ'U'-LLÁH HATH WILLED IT SO! At the time of elections the right to vote is the inalienable right of women, and the entrance of women into all human departments is an irrefutable and incontrovertible question. No soul can retard or prevent it."

('Abdu'l-Bahá, *Paris Talks*, 59.5)

146. "Woman must endeavor then to attain greater perfection, to be man's equal in every respect, to make progress in all in which she has

been backward, so that man will be compelled to acknowledge her equality of capacity and attainment."

('Abdu'l-Bahá, *Paris Talks*, 50.11)

147. "Woman's lack of progress and proficiency has been due to her need of equal education and opportunity. Had she been allowed this equality there is no doubt she would be the counterpart of man in ability and capacity. The happiness of mankind will be realized when women and men coordinate and advance equally, for each is the complement and helpmeet of the other."

('Abdu'l-Bahá, *The Promulgation of Universal Peace*, p. 182)

## E. Education of Children

148. "It is the bounden duty of parents to rear their children to be staunch in faith, the reason being that a child who removeth himself from the religion of God will not act in such a way as to win the good pleasure of his parents and his Lord. For every praiseworthy deed is born out of the light of religion, and lacking this supreme bestowal the child will not turn away from any evil, nor will he draw nigh unto any good."

(Bahá'u'lláh, quoted in *Bahá'í Education: A Compilation*, no. 12)

149. "The fear of God hath ever been the prime factor in the education of His creatures. Well is it with them that have attained thereunto!"

(Bahá'u'lláh, *Epistle to the Son of the Wolf*, p. 27)

150. "Unto every father hath been enjoined the instruction of his son and daughter in the art of reading and writing and in all that hath been laid down in the Holy Tablet. He that putteth away that which is commanded unto him, the Trustees are then to take from him that which is required for their instruction, if he be wealthy, and if not the matter devolveth upon the House of Justice. Verily, have We made it a shelter for the poor and needy. He that bringeth up his son or the son of another, it is as though he hath brought up a son of Mine, upon him rest

My Glory, My loving kindness, My Mercy, that have compassed the world."

(Bahá'u'lláh, quoted in Synopsis and Codification<br>of the Laws and Ordinances of the Kitáb-i-Aqdas, pp. 15–16)

**151.** "It is incumbent upon the children to exert themselves to the utmost in acquiring the art of reading and writing. Writing skills that will provide for urgent needs will be enough for some; and then it is better and more fitting that they should spend their time in studying those branches of knowledge which are of use.

"As for what the Supreme Pen hath previously set down, the reason is that in every art and skill, God loveth the highest perfection."

(Bahá'u'lláh, quoted in Bahá'í Education: A Compilation, no. 20)

**152.** "The mother is the first teacher of the child. For children, at the beginning of life, are fresh and tender as a young twig, and can be trained in any fashion you desire. If you rear the child to be straight, he will grow straight, in perfect symmetry. It is clear that the mother is the first teacher and that it is she who establisheth the character and conduct of the child."

('Abdu'l-Bahá, quoted in Bahá'í Education: A Compilation, no. 96)

**153.** "O ye loving mothers, know ye that in God's sight, the best of all ways to worship Him is to educate the children and train them in all the perfections of humankind; and no nobler deed than this can be imagined."

('Abdu'l-Bahá, Selections from the Writings of 'Abdu'l-Bahá, 114.1)

**154.** "The father must always endeavor to educate his son and to acquaint him with the heavenly teachings. He must give him advice and exhort him at all times, teach him praiseworthy conduct and character, enable him to receive training at school and to be instructed in such arts and sciences as are deemed useful and necessary. In brief, let him instill into his mind the virtues and perfections of the world of humanity. Above all he should continually call to his mind the remembrance of

God so that his throbbing veins and arteries may pulsate with the love of God.

"The son, on the other hand, must show forth the utmost obedience towards his father, and should conduct himself as a humble and a lowly servant. Day and night he should seek diligently to ensure the comfort and welfare of his loving father and to secure his good-pleasure. He must forgo his own rest and enjoyment, and constantly strive to bring gladness to the hearts of his father and mother, that thereby he may attain the good-pleasure of the Almighty and be graciously aided by the hosts of the unseen."

('Abdu'l-Bahá, quoted in a compilation on Family Life dated January 1982 sent by the Universal House of Justice to National Spiritual Assemblies)

**155.** "O handmaids of the Lord! The spiritual assemblage that ye established in that illumined city is most propitious. Ye have made great strides; ye have surpassed the others, have arisen to serve the Holy Threshold, and have won heavenly bestowals. Now with all spiritual zeal must ye gather in that enlightened assemblage and recite the Holy Writings and engage in remembering the Lord. Set ye forth His arguments and proofs. Work ye for the guidance of the women in that land, teach the young girls and the children, so that the mothers may educate their little ones from their earliest days, thoroughly train them, rear them to have a goodly character and good morals, guide them to all the virtues of humankind, prevent the development of any behavior that would be worthy of blame, and foster them in the embrace of Bahá'í education. Thus shall these tender infants be nurtured at the breast of the knowledge of God and His love. Thus shall they grow and flourish, and be taught righteousness and the dignity of humankind, resolution and the will to strive and to endure. Thus shall they learn perseverance in all things, the will to advance, high mindedness and high resolve, chastity and purity of life. Thus shall they be enabled to carry to a successful conclusion whatsoever they undertake.

"Let the mothers consider that whatever concerneth the education of children is of the first importance. Let them put forth every effort in this regard, for when the bough is green and tender it will grow in whatever way ye train it. Therefore is it incumbent upon the mothers to rear their little ones even as a gardener tendeth his young plants. Let them strive by day and by night to establish within their children faith and certitude, the fear of God, the love of the Beloved of the worlds, and all good qualities and traits. Whensoever a mother seeth that her child hath done well, let her praise and applaud him and cheer his heart; and if the slightest undesirable trait should manifest itself, let her counsel the child and punish him, and use means based on reason, even a slight verbal chastisement should this be necessary. It is not, however, permissible to strike a child, or vilify him, for the child's character will be totally perverted if he be subjected to blows or verbal abuse."

('Abdu'l-Bahá, *Selections from the Writings of 'Abdu'l-Bahá*, 95.1–2)

156. "O handmaids of the beauty of Abhá! Your letter hath come, and its perusal brought great joy. Praised be God, the women believers have organized meetings where they will learn how to teach the Faith, will spread the sweet savors of the Teachings and make plans for training the children.

"This gathering must be completely spiritual. That is, the discussions must be confined to marshaling clear and conclusive proofs that the Sun of Truth hath indeed arisen. And further, those present should concern themselves with every means of training the girl children; with teaching the various branches of knowledge, good behavior, a proper way of life, the cultivation of a good character, chastity and constancy, perseverance, strength, determination, firmness of purpose; with household management, the education of children, and whatever especially applieth to the needs of girls—to the end that these girls, reared in the stronghold of all perfections, and with the protection of a goodly character, will, when they themselves become mothers, bring up their children from earliest infancy to have a good character and conduct themselves well.

"Let them also study whatever will nurture the health of the body and its physical soundness, and how to guard their children from disease.

"When matters are thus well arranged, every child will become a peerless plant in the gardens of the Abhá Paradise."

('Abdu'l-Bahá, *Selections from the Writings of 'Abdu'l-Bahá*, 94.1–4)

**157.** "Ye should consider the question of goodly character as of the first importance. It is incumbent upon every father and mother to counsel their children over a long period, and guide them unto those things which lead to everlasting honor.

"Encourage ye the school children, from their earliest years, to deliver speeches of high quality, so that in their leisure time they will engage in giving cogent and effective talks, expressing themselves with clarity and eloquence."

('Abdu'l-Bahá, *Selections from the Writings of 'Abdu'l-Bahá*, 108.1–2)

**158.** "Train your children from their earliest days to be infinitely tender and loving to animals. If an animal be sick, let the children try to heal it, if it be hungry, let them feed it, if thirsty, let them quench its thirst, if weary, let them see that it rests.

"Most human beings are sinners, but the beasts are innocent. Surely those without sin should receive the most kindness and love—all except animals which are harmful, such as bloodthirsty wolves, such as poisonous snakes and similar pernicious creatures, the reason being that kindness to these is an injustice to human beings and to other animals as well."

('Abdu'l-Bahá, *Selections from the Writings of 'Abdu'l-Bahá*, 138.4–5)

**159.** "The art of music is divine and effective. It is the food of the soul and spirit. Through the power and charm of music the spirit of man is uplifted. It has wonderful sway and effect in the hearts of children, for their hearts are pure and melodies have great influence in them. The latent talents with which the hearts of these children are endowed will find expression through the medium of music. Therefore you must exert yourselves to make them proficient; teach them to sing with excellence and effect. It is incumbent upon each child to know something of music, for without knowledge of this art, the melodies of instrument and voice cannot be rightly enjoyed."

('Abdu'l-Bahá, *The Promulgation of Universal Peace*, p. 52)

**160.** "I give you my advice and it is this: Train these children with divine exhortations. From their childhood instill in their hearts the love of God so they may manifest in their lives the fear of God and have confidence in the bestowals of God. Teach them to free themselves from human imperfections and to acquire the divine perfections latent in the heart of man. The life of man is useful if he attains the perfections of man. If he becomes the center of the imperfections of the world of humanity, death is better than life, and nonexistence better than existence. Therefore make ye an effort in order that these children may be rightly trained and educated and that each one of them may attain perfection in the world of humanity. Know ye the value of these children for they are all my children."

(ʻAbduʼl-Bahá, *The Promulgation of Universal Peace*, pp. 53–54)

**161.** "The child must not be oppressed or censured because it is undeveloped; it must be patiently trained."

(ʻAbduʼl-Bahá, *The Promulgation of Universal Peace*, pp. 180–181)

**162.** "With regard to the statement attributed to ʻAbduʼl-Bahá and which you have quoted in your letter regarding a ʻproblem childʼ; these statements of the Master, however true in their substance, should never be given a literal interpretation. ʻAbduʼl-Bahá could have never meant that a child should be left to himself, entirely free. In fact Baháʼí education, just like any other system of education is based on the assumption that there are certain natural deficiencies in every child, no matter how gifted, which his educators, whether his parents, schoolmasters, or his spiritual guides and preceptors should endeavor to remedy. Discipline of some sort, whether physical, moral or intellectual, is indeed indispensable, and no training can be said to be complete and fruitful if it disregards this element. The child when born is far from being perfect. It is not only helpless, but actually is imperfect, and even is naturally inclined towards evil. He should be trained, his natural inclinations harmonized, adjusted and controlled, and if necessary suppressed or regulated, so as to ensure his healthy physical and moral development. Baháʼí parents cannot simply adopt an attitude of nonresistance towards their children . . ."

(Shoghi Effendi, from a letter dated July 9, 1939, written on his behalf to an individual believer)

**163.** "As regards your plans, the Guardian fully approves indeed of your view that no matter how urgent and vital the requirements of the teaching work may be you should under no circumstance neglect the education of your children, as towards them you have an obligation no less sacred than towards the Cause.

"Any plan or arrangement you may arrive at which would combine your two-fold duties toward your family and the Cause, and would permit you to resume active work in the field of pioneer teaching, and also to take good care of your children so as to not jeopardize their future in the Cause would meet with the whole-hearted approval of the Guardian."

(Shoghi Effendi, from a letter dated November 16, 1939,
written on his behalf to an individual believer)

**164.** "The question of the training and education of children in case one of the parents is a non-Bahá'í is one which solely concerns the parents themselves, who should decide about it the way they find best and most conducive to the maintenance of the unity of their family, and to the future welfare of their children. Once the child comes of age, however, he should be given full freedom to choose his religion, irrespective of the wishes and desires of his parents."

(Shoghi Effendi, from a letter dated December 14, 1940, written on his behalf
to the National Spiritual Assembly of India and Burma)

**165.** "That the first teacher of the child is the mother should not be startling, for the primary orientation of the infant is to its mother. This provision of nature in no way minimizes the role of the father in the Bahá'í family. Again, equality of status does not mean identity of function."

(Universal House of Justice, from a letter dated
June 23, 1974, to an individual believer)

## F. Relationships within the Family

**166.** "The parents must exert every effort to rear their offspring to be religious, for should the children not attain this greatest of adornments, they will not obey their parents, which in a certain sense means that they will not obey God. Indeed, such children will show no consideration to anyone, and will do exactly as they please."

(Bahá'u'lláh, quoted in *Bahá'í Education: A Compilation*, no. 14)

**167.** "We have caused thee to return to thy home as a token of Our mercy unto thy mother, inasmuch as We have found her overwhelmed with sorrow. We have enjoined you in the Book 'to worship no one but God and to show kindness to your parents.' Thus hath the one true God spoken and the decree hath been fulfilled by the Almighty, the All-wise. Therefore We have caused Thee to return unto her and unto thy sister, that your mother's eyes may thereby be cheered, and she may be of the thankful.

"Say, O My people! Show honor to your parents and pay homage to them. This will cause blessings to descend upon you from the clouds of the bounty of your Lord, the Exalted, the Great.

"When We learned of her sadness, We directed thee to return unto her, as a token of mercy unto thee from Our presence, and as an admonishment for others.

"Beware lest ye commit that which would sadden the hearts of your fathers and mothers. Follow ye the path of Truth which indeed is a straight path. Should anyone give you a choice between the opportunity to render a service to me and a service to them, choose ye to serve them, and let such service be a path leading you to Me. This is My exhortation and command unto thee. Observe therefore that which thy Lord, the Mighty, the Gracious, hath prescribed unto thee."

(Bahá'u'lláh, quoted in a compilation on Family Life dated January 1982 sent by the Universal House of Justice to National Spiritual Assemblies)

**168.** "The fruits of the tree of existence are trustworthiness, loyalty, truthfulness and purity. After the recognition of the oneness of the Lord, exalted be He, the most important of all duties is to have due regard for the rights of one's parents. This matter hath been mentioned in all the Books of God."

(Bahá'u'lláh, quoted in a compilation on Family Life dated January 1982 sent by the Universal House of Justice to National Spiritual Assemblies)

**169.** "These blessed words were uttered by the Tongue of grandeur in the Land of Mystery (Adrianople), exalted and glorified is His utterance:

"One of the distinguishing characteristics of this most great Dispensation is that the kin of such as have recognized and embraced the truth of this Revelation and have, in the glory of His name, the Sovereign Lord, quaffed the choice, sealed wine from the chalice of the love of the one True God, will, upon their death, if they are outwardly non-believers, be graciously invested with divine forgiveness and partake of the ocean of His Mercy.

"This bounty, however, will be vouchsafed only to such souls as have inflicted no harm upon Him Who is the Sovereign Truth nor upon His loved ones.

"Thus hath it been ordained by Him Who is the Lord of the Throne on high and the Ruler of this world and of the world to come."
(Bahá'u'lláh, quoted in a compilation on Family Life dated January 1982<br>sent by the Universal House of Justice to National Spiritual Assemblies)

**170.** "We have enjoined upon every son to serve his father. Thus have we decreed this command in the Book."
(Bahá'u'lláh, quoted in a compilation on Family Life dated January 1982<br>sent by the Universal House of Justice to National Spiritual Assemblies)

**171.** "If thou wouldst show kindness and consideration to thy parents so that they may feel generally pleased, this would also please Me, for parents must be highly respected and it is essential that they should feel contented, provided they deter thee not from gaining access to the Threshold of the Almighty, nor keep thee back from walking in the way of the Kingdom. Indeed it behooveth them to encourage and spur thee on in this direction."
('Abdu'l-Bahá, quoted in a compilation on Family Life dated January, 1982,<br>sent by the Universal House of Justice to National Spiritual Assemblies)

**172.** "According to the teachings of Bahá'u'lláh, the family being a human unit must be educated according to the rules of sanctity. All the virtues must be taught the family. The integrity of the family bond must be constantly considered and the rights of the individual members must not be transgressed. The rights of the son, the father, the mother, none of them must be transgressed, none of them must be arbitrary. Just as the son has certain obligations to his father, the father likewise has certain obligations to his son. The mother, the sister and other members of the household have their certain prerogatives. All these rights and prerogatives must be conserved, yet the unity of the family must be sustained. The injury of one shall be considered the injury of all; the comfort of each the comfort of all; the honor of one the honor of all."

('Abdu'l-Bahá, *The Promulgation of Universal Peace*, p. 168)

**173.** "The youth must grow and develop and take the place of their fathers, that this abundant grace, in the posterity of each one of the loved ones of God who bore great agonies, may day by day increase, until in the end, it shall yield its fruit on earth and in Heaven."

('Abdu'l-Bahá, quoted in *Bahá'í Education: A Compilation*, no. 103)

**174.** "There are also certain sacred duties of children toward parents, which duties are written in the Book of God, as belonging to God. The (children's) prosperity in this world and the Kingdom depends upon the good pleasure of parents, and without this they will be in manifest loss."

('Abdu'l-Bahá, *Tablets of Abdul-Baha Abbas*, Vol. II, pp. 262–263)

**175.** "O ye dear children!

"Your father is very compassionate, clement and merciful unto you and desireth for you success, prosperity and eternal life in the Kingdom of God. Therefore, it is incumbent upon you, dear children, to seek his good pleasure, to be guided by his guidance, to be drawn by the magnet of the love of God and be brought up in the lap of the love of God; that ye may become beautiful branches in the Garden of El-Abha, verdant and watered by the abundance of the gift of God."

('Abdu'l-Bahá, *Tablets of Abdul-Baha Abbas*, Vol. III, p. 622)

**176.** "O dear one of 'Abdu'l-Bahá! Be the son of thy father and be the fruit of that tree. Be a son that hath been born of his soul and heart and not only of the water and clay. A real son is such an one as hath branched from the spiritual part of a man. I ask God that thou mayest be at all times confirmed and strengthened."

('Abdu'l-Bahá, *Tablets of Abdul-Baha Abbas*, Vol. II, p. 342)

**177.** "Comfort thy mother and endeavor to do what is conducive to the happiness of her heart."

('Abdu'l-Bahá, *Tablets of Abdul-Baha Abbas*, Vol. I, p. 74)

**178.** "You have asked whether a husband would be able to prevent his wife from embracing the divine light or a wife dissuade her husband from gaining entry into the Kingdom of God. In truth neither of them could prevent the other from entering into the Kingdom, unless the husband hath an excessive attachment to the wife or the wife to the husband. Indeed when either of the two worshippeth the other to the exclusion of God, then each could prevent the other from seeking admittance into His Kingdom."

('Abdu'l-Bahá, quoted in a compilation on Family Life dated January 1982
sent by the Universal House of Justice to National Spiritual Assemblies)

**179.** "Regarding thy question about consultation of a father with his son, or a son with his father, in matters of trade and commerce, consultation is one of the fundamental elements of the foundation of the Law of God. Such consultation is assuredly acceptable, whether between father and son, or with others. There is nothing better than this. Man must consult in all things for this will lead him to the depths of each problem and enable him to find the right solution."

('Abdu'l-Bahá, quoted in a compilation on Family Life dated January 1982
sent by the Universal House of Justice to National Spiritual Assemblies)

**180.** "It is one of the essential teachings of the Faith that unity should be maintained in the home. Of course this does not mean that any member of the family has a right to influence the faith of any other member; and if this is realized by all the members then it seems certain that unity would be feasible."

(Shoghi Effendi, from a letter dated July 6, 1952,
written on his behalf to an individual believer)

**181.** "In regard to the question you asked him: he feels sure that, although in some ways you may be a financial burden to your children, it is to them a privilege to look after you; you are their mother and have given them life, and through the bounty of Bahá'u'lláh they are now attracted to His Faith. Anything they do for you is small recompense for all you have done for them."

(Shoghi Effendi, from a letter dated September 20, 1948,<br>written on his behalf to an individual believer)

**182.** "It made him very happy to know of the recent confirmation of your . . . friend, and of her earnest desire to serve and promote the Faith. He will certainly pray on her behalf that she may, notwithstanding the opposition of her parents and relatives, increasingly gain in knowledge and in understanding of the Teachings, and become animated with such zeal as to arise, and bring into the Cause a large number of her former co-religionists.

"Under no circumstances, however, should she allow her parents to become completely alienated from her, but it is her bounden duty to strive, through patient, continued and loving effort, to win their sympathy for the Faith, and even perhaps, to bring about their confirmation . . ."

(Shoghi Effendi, from a letter dated July 6, 1938,<br>written on his behalf to an individual believer)

**183.** "The House of Justice suggests that all statements in the Holy Writings concerning specific areas of the relationship between men and women should be considered in the light of the general principle of equality between the sexes that has been authoritatively and repeatedly enunciated in the Sacred Texts. In one of His Tablets 'Abdu'l-Bahá asserts: 'In this divine age the bounties of God have encompassed the world of women. Equality of men and women, except in some negligible instances, has been fully and categorically announced. Distinctions have been utterly removed.' That men and women differ from one another in certain characteristics and functions is an inescapable fact of nature; the important thing is that 'Abdu'l-Bahá regards such inequalities as remain between the sexes as being 'negligible.'

"The relationship between husband and wife must be viewed in the context of the Bahá'í ideal of family life. Bahá'u'lláh came to bring unity to the world, and a fundamental unity is that of the family. Therefore, one must believe that the Faith is intended to strengthen the family, not weaken it, and one of the keys to the strengthening of unity is loving consultation. The atmosphere within a Bahá'í family as within the community as a whole should express 'the keynote of the Cause of God' which, the beloved Guardian has stated, 'is not dictatorial authority but humble fellowship, not arbitrary power, but the spirit of frank and loving consultation.'

"A family, however, is a very special kind of 'community.' The Research Department has not come across any statements which specifically name the father as responsible for the 'security, progress and unity of the family' . . . but it can be inferred from a number of the responsibilities placed upon him, that the father can be regarded as the 'head' of the family. The members of a family all have duties and responsibilities towards one another and to the family as a whole, and these duties and responsibilities vary from member to member because of their natural relationships. The parents have the inescapable duty to educate their children—but not vice versa; the children have the duty to obey their parents—the parents do not obey the children; the mother—not the father—bears the children, nurses them in babyhood, and is thus their first educator, hence daughters have a prior right to education over sons and, as the Guardian's secretary has written on his behalf, 'The task of bringing up a Bahá'í child, as emphasized time and again in Bahá'í Writings, is the chief responsibility of the mother, whose unique privilege is indeed to create in her home such conditions as 'would be most conducive to both his material and spiritual welfare and advancement. The training which the child first receives through his mother constitutes the strongest foundation for his future development.' A corollary of this responsibility of the mother is her right to be supported by her husband—a husband has no explicit right to be supported by his wife. This principle of the husband's responsibility to provide for and protect the family can be seen applied also in the law in intestacy which provides that the family's dwelling place passes, on the father's death, not to his widow, but to his eldest son; the son at the same time has the responsibility to care for his mother.

"It is in this context of mutual and complementary duties and responsibilities that one should read the Tablet in which 'Abdu'l-Bahá gives the following exhortation:

'O Handmaids of the Self-Sustaining Lord! Exert your efforts so that you may obtain the honor and privilege ordained for women. Undoubtedly the greatest glory of women is servitude at His threshold and submissiveness at His door; it is the possession of a vigilant heart, and praise of the incomparable God; it is heartfelt love towards other handmaids and spotless chastity; it is obedience to and consideration for their husbands and the education and care of their children; and it is tranquillity, and dignity, and perseverance in the remembrance of the Lord, and the utmost enkindlement and attraction.'

"This exhortation to the utmost degree of spirituality and self-abnegation should not be read as a legal definition giving the husband absolute authority over his wife, for, in a letter written to an individual believer on 22 July 1943, the beloved Guardian's secretary wrote on his behalf:

'The Guardian, in his remarks . . . about parents and children, wives' and husbands' relations in America, meant that there is a tendency in that country for children to be too independent of the wishes of their parents and lacking in the respect due to them. Also wives, in some cases, have a tendency to exert an unjust degree of domination over their husbands which, of course, is not right, any more than that the husband should unjustly dominate his wife.'

"In any group, however loving the consultation, there are nevertheless points on which, from time to time, agreement cannot be reached. In a Spiritual Assembly this dilemma is resolved by a majority vote. There can, however, be no majority where only two parties are involved, as in the case of a husband and wife. There are, therefore, times when a wife should defer to her husband, and times when a husband should defer to his wife, but neither should ever unjustly dominate the other. In short, the relationship between husband and wife should be as held forth in the prayer revealed by 'Abdu'l-Bahá which is often read at Bahá'í weddings: 'Verily they are married in obedience to Thy command. Cause them to become the signs of harmony and unity till the end of time.'

"These are all relationships within the family, but there is a much wider sphere of relationship between men and women than in the home, and this too we should consider in the context of Bahá'í society, not in that of past or present social norms. For example, although the mother is the first educator of the child, and the most formative influence in his development, the father also has the responsibility of educating his children, and this responsibility is so weighty that Bahá'u'lláh has stated that a father who fails to exercise it forfeits his rights of fatherhood. Similarly, although the primary responsibility for supporting the family financially is placed upon the husband, this does not by any means imply that the place of women is confined to the home. On the contrary, 'Abdu'l-Bahá has stated:

'In this Revelation of Bahá'u'lláh, the women go neck and neck with men. In no movement will they be left behind. Their rights with men are equal in degree. They will enter all the administrative branches of politics. They will attain in all such a degree as will be considered the very highest station of the world of humanity and will take part in all affairs.'

*(Paris Talks,* [59.5])

and again:

'So it will come to pass that when women participate fully and equally in the affairs of the world, enter confidently and capably the great arena of laws and politics, war will cease; . . .'

*(The Promulgation of Universal Peace,* p. 135)

"In the Tablet of the World, Bahá'u'lláh Himself has envisaged that women as well as men would be breadwinners in stating:

'Everyone, whether man or woman, should hand over to a trusted person a portion of what he or she earneth through trade, agriculture or other occupation, for the training and education of children, to be spent for this purpose with the knowledge of the Trustees of the House of Justice.'

*(Tablets of Bahá'u'lláh,* p. 90)

"A very important element in the attainment of such equality is Bahá'u'lláh's provision that boys and girls must follow essentially the same curriculum in schools."

(Universal House of Justice, from a letter dated December 28, 1980, to the National Spiritual Assembly of New Zealand)

## G. Death

**184. "O SON OF THE SUPREME!**

"I have made death a messenger of joy to thee. Wherefore dost thou grieve? I made the light to shed on thee its splendor. Why dost thou veil thyself therefrom?"

(Bahá'u'lláh, *The Hidden Words*, p. 11)

**185.** "O thou assured soul, thou maidservant of God . . . ! Be not grieved at the death of thy respected husband. He hath, verily, attained the meeting of His Lord at the seat of Truth in the presence of the potent King. Do not suppose that thou hast lost him. The veil shall be lifted and thou shalt behold his face illumined in the Supreme Concourse. Just as God, the Exalted, hath said, 'Him will we surely quicken to a happy life.' Supreme importance should be attached, therefore, not to this first creation but rather to the future life."

('Abdu'l-Bahá, *Selections from the Writings of 'Abdu'l-Bahá*, 165.4)

**186.** "O thou beloved maid-servant of God, although the loss of a son is indeed heart-breaking and beyond the limits of human endurance, yet one who knoweth and understandeth is assured that the son hath not been lost but, rather, hath stepped from this world into another, and she will find him in the divine realm. That reunion shall be for eternity, while in this world separation is inevitable and bringeth with it a burning grief.

"Praise be unto God that thou hast faith, art turning thy face toward the everlasting Kingdom and believest in the existence of a heavenly world. Therefore be thou not disconsolate, do not languish, do not sigh, neither wail nor weep; for agitation and mourning deeply affect his soul in the divine realm.

"That beloved child addresseth thee from the hidden world: 'O thou kind Mother, thank divine Providence that I have been freed from a small and gloomy cage and, like the birds of the meadows, have soared to the divine world—a world which is spacious, illumined, and ever gay and jubilant. Therefore, lament not, O Mother, and be not grieved; I am not of the lost, nor have I been obliterated and destroyed. I have shaken off the mortal form and have raised my banner in this spiritual world. Following this separation is everlasting companionship. Thou shalt find me in the heaven of the Lord, immersed in an ocean of light.'"

('Abdu'l-Bahá, *Selections from the Writings of 'Abdu'l-Bahá*, 171.1–3)

187. "Question.—What is the condition of children who die before attaining the age of discretion, or before the appointed time of birth?

"Answer.—These infants are under the shadow of the favor of God; and as they have not committed any sin, and are not soiled with the impurities of the world of nature, they are the centers of the manifestation of bounty, and the Eye of Compassion will be turned upon them."

('Abdu'l-Bahá, *Some Answered Questions*, pp. 278–279)

188. "The death of that beloved youth and his separation from you have caused the utmost sorrow and grief; for he winged his flight in the flower of his age and the bloom of his youth to the heavenly nest. But he hath been freed from this sorrow-stricken shelter and hath turned his face toward the everlasting nest of the Kingdom, and, being delivered from a dark and narrow world, hath hastened to the sanctified realm of light; therein lieth the consolation of our hearts.

"The inscrutable divine wisdom underlieth such heart-rending occurrences. It is as if a kind gardener transferreth a fresh and tender shrub from a confined place to a wide open area. This transfer is not the cause of the withering, the lessening or the destruction of that shrub; nay, on the contrary, it maketh it to grow and thrive, acquire freshness and delicacy, become green and bear fruit. This hidden secret is well known to the gardener, but those souls who are unaware of this bounty suppose that the gardener, in his anger and wrath, hath uprooted the shrub. Yet to those who are aware, this concealed fact is manifest, and this predestined decree is considered a bounty. Do not feel grieved or disconsolate, therefore, at the ascension of that bird of faithfulness; nay, under all circumstances pray for that youth, supplicating for him forgiveness and the elevation of his station.

"I hope that you will attain the utmost patience, composure and resignation and I entreat and implore at the Threshold of Oneness, begging for forgiveness and pardon. My hope from the infinite bounties of God is that He may shelter this dove of the garden of faith, and cause him to abide on the branch of the Supreme Concourse, that he may sing in the best of melodies the praise and glorification of the Lord of Names and Attributes."

('Abdu'l-Bahá, *Selections from the Writings of 'Abdu'l-Bahá*, 169.1–3)

**189.** "In the next world man will find himself freed from many of the disabilities under which he now suffers. Those who have passed on through death, have a sphere of their own. It is not removed from ours: their work of the Kingdom, is ours; but it is sanctified from what we call time and place. Time with us is measured by the sun. When there is no more sunrise and no more sunset, that kind of time does not exist for man. Those who have ascended have different attributes (conditions) from those who are still on earth, yet there is no real separation.

"In prayer there is a mingling of stations, a mingling of condition. Pray for them as they pray for you."

('Abdu'l-Bahá, *'Abdu'l-Bahá in London*, p. 97)

## H. Work and Finances

**190.** "Whatsoever deterreth you, in this Day, from loving God is nothing but the world. Flee it, that ye may be numbered with the blest. Should a man wish to adorn himself with the ornaments of the earth, to wear its apparels, or partake of the benefits it can bestow, no harm can befall him, if he alloweth nothing whatever to intervene between him and God, for God hath ordained every good thing, whether created in the heavens or in the earth, for such of His servants as truly believe in Him. Eat ye, O people, of the good things which God hath allowed you, and deprive not yourselves from His wondrous bounties. Render thanks and praise unto him, and be of them that are truly thankful."

(Bahá'u'lláh, *Gleanings from the Writings of Bahá'u'lláh*, p. 276)

### 191. "O SON OF MAN!

"Should prosperity befall thee, rejoice not, and should abasement come upon thee, grieve not, for both shall pass away and be no more."

(Bahá'u'lláh, *The Hidden Words*, p. 16)

### 192. "O SON OF BEING!

"If poverty overtake thee, be not sad; for in time the Lord of wealth shall visit thee. Fear not abasement, for glory shall one day rest on thee."

(Bahá'u'lláh, *The Hidden Words*, p. 16)

### 193. "O MY SERVANT!

"The best of men are they that earn a livelihood by their calling and spend upon themselves and upon their kindred for the love of God, the Lord of all worlds."

(Bahá'u'lláh, *The Hidden Words*, p. 51)

### 194. "O thou servant of the One true God! In this universal dispensation man's wondrous craftsmanship is reckoned as worship of the Resplendent Beauty. Consider what a bounty and blessing it is that craftsmanship is regarded as worship. In former times, it was believed that such skills were tantamount to ignorance, if not a misfortune, hindering man from drawing nigh unto God. Now consider how His infinite bestowals and abundant favors have changed hell-fire into blissful paradise, and a heap of dark dust into a luminous garden.

"It behooveth the craftsmen of the world at each moment to offer a thousand tokens of gratitude at the Sacred Threshold, and to exert their highest endeavor and diligently pursue their professions so that their efforts may produce that which will manifest the greatest beauty and perfection before the eyes of all men."

('Abdu'l-Bahá, *Selections from the Writings of 'Abdu'l-Bahá*, 127.1–2)

**195.** "Thy letter was received. I hope that thou mayest be protected and assisted under the providence of the True one, be occupied always in mentioning the Lord and display effort to complete thy profession. Thou must endeavor greatly so that thou mayest become unique in thy profession and famous in those parts, because attaining perfection in one's profession in this merciful period is considered to be worship of God. And whilst thou art occupied with thy profession, thou canst remember the True One."

('Abdu'l-Bahá, *Selections from the Writings of 'Abdu'l-Bahá*, 128.1)

**196.** "Some men's lives are solely occupied with the things of this world; their minds are so circumscribed by exterior manners and traditional interests that they are blind to any other realm of existence, to the spiritual significance of all things! They think and dream of earthly fame, of material progress. Sensuous delights and comfortable surroundings bound their horizon, their highest ambitions center in success of worldly conditions and circumstances! They curb not their lower propensities; they eat, drink and sleep! Like the animal, they have no thought beyond their own physical well-being. It is true that these necessities must be dispatched. Life is a load which must be carried on while we are on earth, but the cares of the lower things of life should not be allowed to monopolize all the thoughts and aspirations of a human being. The heart's ambitions should ascend to a more glorious goal, mental activity should rise to higher levels! Men should hold in their souls the vision of celestial perfection, and there prepare a dwelling-place for the inexhaustible bounty of the Divine Spirit.

"Let your ambition be the achievement on earth of a Heavenly civilization! I ask for you the supreme blessing, that you may be so filled with the vitality of the Heavenly Spirit that you may be the cause of life to the world."

('Abdu'l-Bahá, *Paris Talks*, 31.9–10)

**197.** "If a man is successful in his business, art, or profession he is thereby enabled to increase his physical wellbeing and to give his body the amount of ease and comfort in which it delights. All around us today we see how man surrounds himself with every modern convenience and luxury, and denies nothing to the physical and material side of his nature. But, take heed, lest in thinking too earnestly of the things of the body you forget the things of the soul: for material advantages do not elevate the spirit of man. Perfection in worldly things is a joy to the body of a man but in no wise does it glorify his soul.

"It may be that a man who has every material benefit, and who lives surrounded by all the greatest comfort modern civilization can give him, is denied the all important gift of the Holy Spirit.

"It is indeed a good and praiseworthy thing to progress materially, but in so doing, let us not neglect the more important spiritual progress, and close our eyes to the Divine light shining in our midst."

('Abdu'l-Bahá, *Paris Talks*, 19.3–5)

**198.** "We must be like the fountain or spring that is continually emptying itself of all that it has and is continually being refilled from an invisible source. To be continually giving out for the good of our fellows undeterred by the fear of poverty and reliant on the unfailing bounty of the Source of all wealth and all good—this is the secret of right living."

(Shoghi Effendi, quoted in *Bahá'í Funds and Contributions*, p. 16)

**199.** "Even though Shoghi Effendi would urge every believer to sacrifice as much as possible for the sake of contributing towards the fund of the National Assembly, yet he would discourage the friends to incur debts for that purpose. We are asked to give what we have, not what we do not possess, especially if such an act causes suffering to others. In such matters we should use judgment and wisdom and take into our confidence other devoted Bahá'ís."

(Shoghi Effendi, quoted in *Bahá'í Funds and Contributions*, p. 10)

## I. Hospitality

**200.** "Blessed is the house that hath attained unto My tender mercy, wherein My remembrance is celebrated, and which is ennobled by the presence of My loved ones, who have proclaimed My praise, cleaved fast to the cord of My grace and been honored by chanting My verses.

Verily they are the exalted servants whom God hath extolled in the Qayyúmu'l-Asmá' and other scriptures. Verily He is the All-Hearing, the Answerer, He Who perceiveth all things."

(Bahá'u'lláh, quoted in a compilation on Family Life dated January 1982 sent from the Universal House of Justice to National Spiritual Assemblies)

201. ". . . consort with the followers of all religions in a spirit of friendliness and fellowship . . . They that are endued with sincerity and faithfulness should associate with all the peoples and kindreds of the earth with joy and radiance, inasmuch as consorting with people hath promoted and will continue to promote unity and concord, which in turn are conducive to the maintenance of order in the world and to the regeneration of nations. Blessed are such as hold fast to the cord of kindliness and tender mercy and are free from animosity and hatred."

(Bahá'u'lláh, *Tablets of Bahá'u'lláh*, pp. 35–36)

202. "O MY FRIENDS!

"Walk ye in the ways of the good pleasure of the Friend, and know that His pleasure is in the pleasure of His creatures. That is: no man should enter the house of his friend save at his friend's pleasure, nor lay hands upon his treasures nor prefer his own will to his friend's, and in no wise seek an advantage over him. Ponder this, ye that have insight!"

(Bahá'u'lláh, *The Hidden Words*, p. 37)

203. "O my God! let the outpourings of Thy bounty and blessings descend upon homes whose inmates have embraced Thy Faith, as a token of Thy grace and as a mark of loving-kindness from Thy presence."

(The Báb, *Selections from the Writings of the Báb*, p. 200)

204. "My home is the home of peace. My home is the home of joy and delight. My home is the home of laughter and exaltation. Whoever enters through the portals of this home, must go out with gladsome heart. This is the home of light; whoever enters here must become illumined."

('Abdu'l-Bahá, quoted in *Star of the West*, Vol. XX, No. 2, p. 52)

**205.** "Treat all thy friends and relatives, even strangers, with a spirit of utmost love and kindliness."

('Abdu'l-Bahá, quoted in a compilation on Family Life dated January 1982
sent by the Universal House of Justice to National Spiritual Assemblies)

**206.** "Wherefore must the loved ones of God associate in affectionate fellowship with stranger and friend alike, showing forth to all the utmost loving-kindness, disregarding the degree of their capacity, never asking whether they deserve to be loved. In every instance let the friends be considerate and infinitely kind."

('Abdu'l-Bahá, *Selections from the Writings of 'Abdu'l-Bahá*, 8.8)

**207.** "I beseech God to graciously make of thy home a center for the diffusion of the light of divine guidance, for the dissemination of the Words of God and for enkindling at all times the fire of love in the hearts of His faithful servants and maidservants. Know thou of a certainty that every house wherein the anthem of praise is raised to the Realm of Glory in celebration of the Name of God is indeed a heavenly home, and one of the gardens of delight in the Paradise of God."

('Abdu'l-Bahá, quoted in a compilation on Family Life dated January 1982
sent by the Universal House of Justice to National Spiritual Assemblies)

**208.** "This is in truth a Bahá'í house. Every time such a house or meeting place is founded it becomes one of the greatest aids to the general development of the town and country to which it belongs. It encourages the growth of learning and science and is known for its intense spirituality and for the love it spreads among the peoples."

('Abdu'l-Bahá, *Paris Talks*, 24.1)

## J. Relationship with Bahá'í Institutions and Community

**209.** "The first condition is firmness in the Covenant of God. For the power of the Covenant will protect the Cause of Bahá'u'lláh from the doubts of the people of error. It is the fortified fortress of the Cause of God and the firm pillar of the religion of God. Today no power can conserve the oneness of the Bahá'í world save the Covenant of God; otherwise differences like unto a most great tempest will encompass the Bahá'í world. It is evident that the axis of the oneness of the world of humanity is the power of the Covenant and nothing else . . . Therefore, in the beginning one must make his steps firm in the Covenant so that the confirmations of Bahá'u'lláh may encircle from all sides, the cohorts of the Supreme Concourse may become the supporters and the helpers, and the exhortations and advices of 'Abdu'l-Bahá, like unto the pictures engraved on stone, may remain permanent and ineffaceable in the tablets of the hearts."

('Abdu'l-Bahá, *Tablets of the Divine Plan*, 8.8)

**210.** "There are certain pillars which have been established as the unshakable supports of the Faith of God. The mightiest of these is learning and the use of the mind, the expansion of consciousness, and insight into the realities of the universe and the hidden mysteries of Almighty God.

"To promote knowledge is thus an inescapable duty imposed on every one of the friends of God. It is incumbent upon that Spiritual Assembly, that assemblage of God, to exert every effort to educate the children, so that from infancy they will be trained in Bahá'í conduct and the ways of God, and will, even as young plants, thrive and flourish in the soft-flowing waters that are the counsels and admonitions of the Blessed Beauty."

('Abdu'l-Bahá, *Selections from the Writings of 'Abdu'l-Bahá*, 97.1–2)

**211.** "And now as I look into the future, I hope to see the friends at all times, in every land, and of every shade of thought and character, voluntarily and joyously rallying round their local and in particular their national centers of activity, upholding and promoting their interests with complete unanimity and contentment, with perfect understanding, genuine enthusiasm, and sustained vigor. This indeed is the one joy and yearning of my life, for it is the fountain-head from which all future blessings will flow, the broad foundation upon which the security of the Divine Edifice must ultimately rest."

(Shoghi Effendi, *Bahá'í Administration*, p. 67)

**212.** "There is a time set aside at the 19 Day Feasts for the Community to express its views and make suggestions to its Assembly; the Assembly and the believers should look forward to this happy period of discussion, and neither fear it nor suppress it."

(Shoghi Effendi, from a letter dated June 20, 1949, written on his behalf to the National Spiritual Assembly of Germany and Austria)

**213.** "He was very sorry to hear that you have had so many tests in your Bahá'í life. There is no doubt that many of them are due to your own nature. In other words, if we are very sensitive, or if we are in some way brought up in a different environment from the Bahá'ís amongst whom we live, we naturally see things differently and may feel them more acutely; and the other side of it is that the imperfections of our fellow-Bahá'ís can be a great trial to us.

"He feels that, if you close your eyes to the failings of others, and fix your love and prayers upon Bahá'u'lláh, you will have the strength to weather this storm, and will be much better for it in the end, spiritually. Although you suffer, you will gain a maturity that will enable you to be of greater help to both your fellow-Bahá'ís and your children."

(Shoghi Effendi, from a letter dated April 5, 1956, written on his behalf to an individual believer)

**214.** "The friends must be patient with each other and must realize that the Cause is still in its infancy and its institutions are not yet functioning perfectly. The greater the patience, the loving understanding and the forbearance the believers show towards each other and their shortcomings, the greater will be the progress of the whole Bahá'í community at large."

(Shoghi Effendi, from a letter dated February 27, 1943, written on his behalf to an individual believer)

**215.** "The greatest need it seems everywhere inside the Cause is to impress upon the friends the need for love among them. There is a tendency to mix up the functions of the Administration and try to apply it in individual relationships, which is abortive, because the Assembly is a nascent House of Justice and is supposed to administer, according to the

Teachings, the affairs of the community. But individuals toward each other are governed by love, unity, forgiveness and a sin-covering eye. Once the friends grasp this they will get along much better, but they keep playing Spiritual Assembly to each other and expect the Assembly to behave like an individual . . ."

(Shoghi Effendi, from a letter dated October 5, 1950,
written on his behalf to an individual believer)

**216.** "When criticism and harsh words arise within a Bahá'í community, there is no remedy except to put the past behind one, and persuade all concerned to turn over a new leaf, and for the sake of God and His Faith refrain from mentioning the subjects which have led to misunderstanding and inharmony. The more the friends argue back and forth and maintain, each side, that their point of view is the right one the worse the whole situation becomes.

"When we see the condition the world is in today, we must surely forget these utterly insignificant internal disturbances, and rush, unitedly, to the rescue of humanity. You should urge your fellow-Bahá'ís to take this point of view, and to support you in a strong effort to suppress every critical thought and every harsh word, in order to let the spirit of Bahá'u'lláh flow into the entire community, and unite it in His love and His service."

(Shoghi Effendi, from a letter dated February 16, 1951,
written on his behalf to an individual believer)

**217.** "We must realize our imperfection and not permit ourselves to get too upset over the unfortunate things which occur, sometimes in Conventions, sometimes in Assemblies or on Committees, etc. Such things are essentially superficial and in time will be outgrown."

(Shoghi Effendi, from a letter dated March 17, 1943,
written on his behalf to an individual believer)

**218.** "He feels, in regard to your family problems, that you should take these matters up with your assembly, if you desire advice; one of the duties of these assemblies is to advise and aid the friends, and it is your privilege to turn to your Assembly."

(Shoghi Effendi, from a letter dated April 10, 1947,
written on his behalf to an individual believer)

**219.** "The divinely ordained institution of the Local Spiritual Assembly operates at the first levels of human society and is the basic administrative unit of Bahá'u'lláh's World Order. It is concerned with individuals and families whom it must constantly encourage to unite in a distinctive Bahá'í society, vitalized and guarded by the laws, ordinances and principles of Bahá'u'lláh's Revelation. It protects the Cause of God; it acts as the loving shepherd of the Bahá'í flock."

(Universal House of Justice, in its Message to the Bahá'ís of the World, launching the Five Year Plan, Naw-Rúz, 1974)

**220.** "When a believer has a problem concerning which he must make a decision, he has several courses open to him. If it is a matter that affects the interests of the Faith he should consult with the appropriate Assembly or committee, but individuals have many problems which are purely personal and there is no obligation to take such problems to the institutions of the Faith: indeed, it is better if the friends will not burden their Assemblies with personal problems that they can solve by themselves.

"A Bahá'í who has a problem may wish to make his own decision upon it after prayer and after weighing all the aspects of it in his own mind; he may prefer to seek the counsel of individual friends or of professional counselors such as his doctor or lawyer so that he can consider such advice when making his decision; or in a case where several people are involved, such as a family situation, he may want to gather together those who are affected so that they may arrive at a collective decision. There is also no objection whatever to a Bahá'í asking a group of people to consult together on a problem facing him.

"It should be borne in mind that all consultation is aimed at arriving at a solution to a problem and is quite different from the sort of group baring of the soul that is popular in some circles these days and which borders on the kind of confession that is forbidden in the Faith. On the subject of confession the Guardian's secretary wrote on his behalf to an individual believer: 'We are forbidden to confess to any person, as do the Catholics to their priests, our sins and shortcomings, or to do so in public, as some religious sects do. However, if we spontaneously desire to acknowledge we have been wrong in something, or that we have some fault of character, and ask another person's forgiveness or pardon, we are quite free to do so. The Guardian wants to point out, however, that we are not obliged to do so. It rests entirely with the individual.'"

(Universal House of Justice, from a letter dated March 19, 1973, to the National Spiritual Assembly of Canada)

221. "The friends are called upon to give their whole-hearted support and cooperation to the Local Spiritual Assembly, first by voting for the membership and then by energetically pursuing its plans and programs, by turning to it in time of trouble or difficulty, by praying for its success and taking delight in its rise to influence and honor. This great prize, this gift of God within each community must be cherished, nurtured, loved, assisted, obeyed and prayed for.

"Such a firmly founded, busy and happy community life as is envisioned when Local Spiritual Assemblies are truly effective, will provide a firm home foundation from which the friends may derive courage and strength and loving support in bearing the Divine Message to their fellow-men and conforming their lives to its benevolent rule."

(Universal House of Justice, in its Message to the Bahá'ís of the World, launching the Five Year Plan, Naw-Rúz, 1974)

## K. Family Life and Bahá'í Service

222. "Praised be God, ye two have demonstrated the truth of your words by your deeds, and have won the confirmation of the Lord God. Every day at first light, ye gather the Bahá'í children together and teach them the communes and prayers. This is a most praiseworthy act, and bringeth joy to the children's hearts: that they should, at every morn, turn their faces toward the Kingdom and make mention of the Lord and praise His Name, and in the sweetest of voices, chant and recite.

"These children are even as young plants, and teaching them the prayers is as letting the rain pour down upon them, that they may wax tender and fresh, and the soft breezes of the love of God may blow over them, making them to tremble with joy."

('Abdu'l-Bahá, Selections from the Writings of 'Abdu'l-Bahá, 115.2–3)

**223.** "A truly Bahá'í home is a true fortress upon which the Cause can rely while planning its campaigns. If . . . and . . . love each other and would like to marry, Shoghi Effendi does not wish them to think that by doing so they are depriving themselves of the privilege of service; in fact such a union will enhance their ability to serve. There is nothing more beautiful than to have young Bahá'ís marry and found truly Bahá'í homes, the type Bahá'u'lláh wishes them to be. Please give them both the Guardian's loving greetings."

(Shoghi Effendi, from a letter dated November 6, 1932,
written on his behalf to an individual believer)

**224.** "It is our duty and privilege to translate the love and devotion we have for our beloved Cause into deeds and actions that will be conducive to the highest good of mankind."

(Shoghi Effendi, from a letter dated November 20, 1924, to an individual believer)

**225.** "Bahá'ís should seek to be many-sided, normal and well balanced, mentally and spiritually. We must not give the impression of being fanatics but at the same time we must live up to our principles."

(Shoghi Effendi, from a letter dated March 12, 1946,
written on his behalf to an individual believer)

**226.** "Surely Shoghi Effendi would like to see you and the other friends give their whole time and energy to the Cause, for we are in great need for competent workers, but the home is an institution that Bahá'u'lláh has come to strengthen and not to weaken. Many unfortunate things have happened in Bahá'í homes just for neglecting this point. Serve the Cause but also remember your duties towards your home. It is for you to find the balance and see that neither makes you neglect the other. We would have many more husbands in the Cause were the wives more thoughtful and moderate in their Bahá'í activities."

(Shoghi Effendi, from a letter dated May 14, 1929,
written on his behalf to an individual believer)

**227.** "The Guardian has long felt that the American Bahá'ís are not, in some cases, living up to the ideal of marriage set forth by Bahá'-

u'lláh. They are prone to being influenced by the current light and selfish attitude of the people towards the marriage bond. Consequently when he sees you are successfully living up to the Bahá'í standard, putting your best into it and preserving this sacred tie you have with your husband, he is very happy indeed. He hopes you will be in a position to be an example to others. For he disapproves of the way some Bahá'ís, in the name of serving the Cause, disencumber themselves of their husbands, or go and get new ones!"

(Shoghi Effendi, from a letter dated April 2, 1950,
written on his behalf to an individual believer)

228. "The Guardian, in view of the fact that your husband does not really wish to be separated from you, but on the contrary is desirous of keeping your marriage together, feels that you, as a Bahá'í, have no right to destroy it because of your desire to serve the Faith.

"Marriage is a very sacred institution. Bahá'u'lláh said its purpose is to promote unity. If the friends neglect, for the sake of the Cause, this institution, they place the Faith in a poor light before the public. In these days the people of the world are so immoral, and treat the marriage institution so lightly; and we, as Bahá'ís, in contrast to the people of the world, are trying to create a high moral standard and reinstate the sanctity of marriage.

"If your husband will allow you to do a certain amount of teaching work, and occasionally travel in the interests of the Faith, all the better; but he does not think the Faith should be made the thing which destroys your family life."

(Shoghi Effendi, from a letter dated June 6, 1954,
written on his behalf to an individual believer)

229. "Your sons, even though they will not be able at first to serve with you in pioneering, are certainly helping you to do so because of their devoted spirit and their complete cooperation. Life at best is so full of unexpected vicissitudes that leaving your boys at home does not, he feels, present any added risks. They are devoted to the Cause and will no doubt be inspired by your example."

(Shoghi Effendi, from a letter dated August 10, 1953,
written on his behalf to an individual believer)

**230.** "Your responsibility towards your son and your husband is very great, and the Guardian hopes your work will soon reach a point where you can return, at least for some time, to them, and give them that love and encouragement which is a woman's great contribution to home life."

(Shoghi Effendi, from a letter dated August 5, 1949,
written on his behalf to an individual believer)

**231.** "He has noted with feelings of genuine admiration your longing to serve in the field of pioneer teaching, but is sorry to hear that your domestic circumstances do not permit you to carry out this dear wish of your heart.

"While he heartily appreciates your eagerness to labor for the Faith in distant and hitherto unopened territories, he feels that, in view of your husband's opposition, and also in consideration of the need of your children for your close help and guidance, you should, for the present, endeavor instead to work in virgin localities in the vicinity of . . . or of the adjoining towns."

(Shoghi Effendi, from a letter dated November 7, 1940,
written on his behalf to an individual believer)

**232.** "Encourage within families, the practice of daily prayer and reading of the Holy Writings."

(Universal House of Justice, from a letter dated
January, 1981, to the Bahá'ís of Canada)

**233.** "In considering the problems that you and your wife are experiencing, the House of Justice points out that the unity of your family should take priority over any other consideration. Bahá'u'lláh came to bring unity to the world, and a fundamental unity is that of the family. Therefore, we must believe that the Faith is intended to strengthen the family, not weaken it. For example, service to the Cause should not produce neglect of the family. It is important for you to arrange your time so that your family life is harmonious and your household receives the attention it requires."

(Universal House of Justice, from a letter dated
August 1, 1978, to an individual believer)

**234.** "Although Bahá'í services should be undertaken with a spirit of sacrifice, one cannot lose sight of the importance given in our Holy Writings to the responsibilities placed on parents in relationship to their children, as well as to the duties of children towards their parents."

(Universal House of Justice, from a letter dated
November 19, 1978, to an individual believer)

## L. Prayers
## For Expectant Mothers

**235.** "My Lord! My Lord! I praise Thee and I thank Thee for whereby Thou hast favored Thine humble maidservant, Thy slave be-seeching and supplicating Thee, because Thou hast verily guided her unto Thine obvious Kingdom and caused her to hear Thine exalted Call in the contingent world and to behold Thy Signs which prove the appearance of Thy victorious reign over all things.

"O my Lord, I dedicate that which is in my womb unto Thee. Then cause it to be a praiseworthy child in Thy Kingdom and a fortu-nate one by Thy favor and Thy generosity; to develop and to grow up under the charge of Thine education. Verily, Thou art the Gracious! Verily, Thou art the Lord of Great Favor!"

('Abdu'l-Bahá, *Bahá'í Prayers*, U.S. 1982, pp. 66–67)

## For Infants

**236.** "Praised be Thou, O Lord my God! Graciously grant that this infant be fed from the breast of Thy tender mercy and loving provi-dence and be nourished with the fruit of Thy celestial trees. Suffer him not to be committed to the care of anyone save Thee, inasmuch as Thou, Thyself, through the potency of Thy sovereign will and power, didst create and call him into being. There is none other God but Thee, the Almighty, the All-Knowing.

"Lauded art Thou, O my Best Beloved, waft over him the sweet savors of Thy transcendent bounty and the fragrances of Thy holy be-stowals. Enable him then to seek shelter beneath the shadow of Thy most exalted name, O Thou Who holdest in Thy grasp the kingdom of names and attributes. Verily Thou art potent to do what Thou willest, and Thou art indeed the Mighty, the Exalted, the Ever-Forgiving, the Gracious, the Generous, the Merciful."

(Bahá'u'lláh, *Bahá'í Prayers and Tablets for the Young*, p. 3)

**237.** "O Thou peerless Lord! Let this suckling babe be nursed from the breast of Thy loving-kindness, guard it within the cradle of Thy safety and protection and grant that it be reared in the arms of Thy tender affection."

('Abdu'l-Bahá, *Bahá'í Prayers and Tablets for the Young*, p. 6)

## For Children

**238.** "O Thou pure God! I am a little child; grant that the breast of Thy loving-kindness be the breast that I cherish; suffer me to be nourished with the honey and the milk of Thy love; rear me in the bosom of Thy knowledge, and bestow upon me nobility and wisdom while I am still a child.

"O Thou the Self-Sufficing God! Make me a confidant of the Kingdom of the Unseen. Verily, Thou art the Mighty, the Powerful."

('Abdu'l-Bahá, *Bahá'í Prayers and Tablets for the Young*, p. 9)

**239.** "O Lord! Graciously assist this child to grow and be quickened in the meads of Thy tender affection. Thou art verily the Bestower, the Merciful, the Compassionate."

('Abdu'l-Bahá, *Bahá'í Prayers and Tablets for the Young*, p. 25)

**240.** "O God, guide me, protect me, make of me a shining lamp and a brilliant star. Thou art the Mighty and the Powerful."

('Abdu'l-Bahá, *Bahá'í Prayers*, U.S. 1982, p. 37)

## For Youth

**241.** "O Lord! Make this youth radiant and confer Thy bounty upon this poor creature. Bestow upon him knowledge, grant him added strength at the break of every morn and guard him within the shelter of Thy protection so that he may be freed from error, may devote himself to the service of Thy Cause, may guide the wayward, lead the hapless, free the captives and awaken the heedless, that all may be blessed with Thy remembrance and praise. Thou art the Mighty and the Powerful."

('Abdu'l-Bahá, *Bahá'í Prayers and Tablets for the Young*, p. 11)

## For Parents

**242.** "It is seemly that the servant should, after each prayer, supplicate God to bestow mercy and forgiveness upon his parents. Thereupon God's call will be raised: 'Thousand upon thousand of what thou hast asked for thy parents shall be thy recompense!' Blessed is he who remembereth his parents when communing with God. There is, verily, no God but Him, the Mighty, the Well-Beloved."

(The Báb, *Selections from the Writings of the Báb*, p. 94)

**243.** "O Lord! In this Most Great Dispensation Thou dost accept the intercession of children in behalf of their parents. This is one of the special infinite bestowals of this Dispensation. Therefore, O Thou kind Lord, accept the request of this Thy servant at the threshold of Thy singleness and submerge his father in the ocean of Thy grace, because this son hath arisen to render Thee service and is exerting effort at all times in the pathway of Thy love. Verily, Thou art the Giver, the Forgiver and the Kind!"

('Abdu'l-Bahá, *Bahá'í Prayers*, U.S. 1982, p. 65)

## For Families

**244.** "Glory be unto Thee, O Lord my God! I beg Thee to forgive me and those who support Thy Faith. Verily, Thou art the sovereign Lord, the Forgiver, the Most Generous. O my God! Enable such ser-

vants of Thine as are deprived of knowledge to be admitted into Thy
Cause; for once they learn of Thee, they bear witness to the truth of the
Day of Judgment and do not dispute the revelations of Thy bounty.
Send down upon them the tokens of Thy grace, and grant them, wher-
ever they reside, a liberal share of that which Thou hast ordained for the
pious among Thy servants. Thou art in truth the Supreme Ruler, the
All-Bounteous, the Most Benevolent.

"O my God! Let the outpourings of Thy bounty and blessings
descend upon homes whose inmates have embraced Thy Faith, as a
token of Thy grace and as a mark of loving-kindness from Thy presence. Verily unsurpassed art Thou in granting forgiveness. Should Thy
bounty be withheld from anyone, how could he be reckoned among the
followers of the Faith in Thy Day?

"Bless me, O my God, and those who will believe in Thy signs on
the appointed Day, and such as cherish my love in their hearts—a love
which Thou dost instill into them. Verily, Thou art the Lord of righteousness, the Most Exalted."

(The Báb, *Selections from the Writings of the Báb*, p. 200)

245. "I beg Thy forgiveness, O my God, and implore pardon after
the manner Thou wishest Thy servants to direct themselves to Thee. I
beg of Thee to wash away our sins as befitteth Thy Lordship, and to
forgive me, my parents, and those who in Thy estimation have entered
the abode of Thy love in a manner which is worthy of Thy transcendent
sovereignty and well beseemeth the glory of Thy celestial power.

"O my God! Thou hast inspired my soul to offer its supplication
to Thee, and but for Thee, I would not call upon Thee. Lauded and
glorified art Thou; I yield Thee praise inasmuch as Thou didst reveal
Thyself unto me, and I beg Thee to forgive me, since I have fallen short
in my duty to know Thee and have failed to walk in the path of Thy
love."

(The Báb, *Selections from the Writings of the Báb*, p. 210)

## For Marriage

246. "He is the Bestower, the Bounteous!
"Praise be to God, the Ancient, the Ever-Abiding, the Changeless,

the Eternal! He Who hath testified in His Own Being that verily He is the One, the Single, the Untrammeled, the Exalted. We bear witness that verily there is no God but Him, acknowledging His oneness, confessing His singleness. He hath ever dwelt in unapproachable heights, in the summits of His loftiness, sanctified from the mention of aught save Himself, free from the description of aught but Him.

"And when He desired to manifest grace and beneficence to men, and to set the world in order, He revealed observances and created laws; among them He established the law of marriage, made it as a fortress for well-being and salvation, and enjoined it upon us in that which was sent down out of the heaven of sanctity in His Most Holy Book. He saith, great is His glory: 'Enter into wedlock, O people, that ye may bring forth one who will make mention of Me amid My servants. This is My bidding unto you; hold fast to it as an assistance to yourselves.'"

(Bahá'u'lláh, *Bahá'í Prayers*, U.S. 1982, pp. 104–105)

247. "Glory be unto Thee, O my God! Verily, this Thy servant and this Thy maidservant have gathered under the shadow of Thy mercy and they are united through Thy favor and generosity. O Lord! Assist them in this Thy world and Thy kingdom and destine for them every good through Thy bounty and grace. O Lord! Confirm them in Thy servitude and assist them in Thy service. Suffer them to become the signs of Thy Name in Thy world and protect them through Thy bestowals which are inexhaustible in this world and the world to come. O Lord! They are supplicating the kingdom of Thy mercifulness and invoking the realm of Thy singleness. Verily, they are married in obedience to Thy command. Cause them to become the signs of harmony and unity until the end of time. Verily, Thou art the Omnipotent, the Omnipresent and the Almighty!"

('Abdu'l-Bahá, *Bahá'í Prayers*, U.S. 1982, p. 107)

248. "O my Lord, O my Lord! These two bright moons are wedded in Thy love, conjoined in servitude to Thy Holy Threshold, united in ministering to Thy Cause. Make Thou this marriage to be as threading lights of Thine abounding grace, O my Lord, the All-Merciful, and luminous rays of Thy bestowals, O Thou the Beneficent, the Ever-Giving, that there may branch out from this great tree boughs that will grow

green and flourishing through the gifts that rain down from Thy clouds of grace.

"Verily, Thou art the Generous. Verily, Thou art the Almighty. Verily, Thou art the Compassionate, the All-Merciful."

('Abdu'l-Bahá, *Bahá'í Prayers*, U.S. 1982, pp. 107–108)

**249.** "He is God!

"O peerless Lord! In Thine almighty wisdom Thou hast enjoined marriage upon the peoples, that the generations of men may succeed one another in this contingent world, and that ever, so long as the world shall last, they may busy themselves at the Threshold of Thy oneness with servitude and worship, with salutation, adoration and praise. 'I have not created spirits and men, but that they should worship me.' Wherefore, wed Thou in the heaven of Thy mercy these two birds of the nest of Thy love, and make them the means of attracting perpetual grace; that from the union of these two seas of love a wave of tenderness may surge and cast the pearls of pure and goodly issue on the shore of life. 'He hath let loose the two seas, that they meet each other: Between them is a barrier which they overpass not. Which then of the bounties of your Lord will ye deny? From each He bringeth up greater and lesser pearls.'

"O Thou kind Lord! Make Thou this marriage to bring forth coral and pearls. Thou art verily the All-Powerful, the Most Great, the Ever-Forgiving."

('Abdu'l-Bahá, *Bahá'í Prayers*, U.S. 1982, pp. 105–106)

**250.** "O God, my God! This Thy handmaid is calling upon Thee, trusting in Thee, turning her face unto Thee, imploring Thee to shed Thy heavenly bounties upon her, and to disclose unto her Thy spiritual mysteries, and to cast upon her the lights of Thy Godhead.

"O my Lord! Make the eyes of my husband to see. Rejoice Thou his heart with the light of the knowledge of Thee, draw Thou his mind unto Thy luminous beauty, cheer Thou his spirit by revealing unto him Thy manifest splendors.

"O my Lord! Lift Thou the veil from before his sight. Rain down Thy plenteous bounties upon him, intoxicate him with the wine of love for Thee, make him one of Thy angels whose feet walk upon this earth even as their souls are soaring through the high heavens. Cause him to become a brilliant lamp, shining out with the light of Thy wisdom in the midst of Thy people.

"Verily Thou art the Precious, the Ever-Bestowing, the Open of Hand."

('Abdu'l-Bahá, *Selections from the Writings of 'Abdu'l-Bahá*, 90.1–4)